NUMBER 289

THE ENGLISH
EXPERIENCE

ITS RECORD IN EARLY PRINTED BOOKS
PUBLISHED IN FACSIMILE

LA RAMEE

THE LATINE GRAMMAR
OF P. RAMVS

LONDON 1585

DA CAPO PRESS
THEATRVM ORBIS TERRARVM LTD.
AMSTERDAM 1971 NEW YORK

The publishers acknowledge their gratitude
to the Syndics of Cambridge University Library
for their permission to reproduce
the Library's copy

(Shelfmark: Syn.8.58.51)

S.T.C. No. 15252
Collation: A-I^8, K^4; A-D^8

Published in 1971 by
Theatrum Orbis Terrarum Ltd.,
O.Z. Voorburgwal 85, Amsterdam

&

Da Capo Press
- a division of Plenum Publishing Corporation -
227 West 17th Street, New York, 10011
Printed in the Netherlands
ISBN 90 221 0289 0

IESV
CHRISTO

DVCE ET
AVSPICE.

THE

LATINE

GRAMMAR OF
P. RAMVS:
Translated into
English.

❧ *Seene and allowed.*

AT LONDON;

Printed by Robert Wal-
de-grave: 1585.

THE FIRST

Booke of P. Ramus

his Grammer.

CAP. I.

Of Letters.

Grammar is the art to speak well: the Latine Grammar teacheth to speak Latine wel, the Greeke Grammar to speake Greeke well, the Hebrue Grammar to speak Hebrue well: Ther are two parts of Grammar; *Etymologie,* and *Sintaxe.* *Etymologie,* is the first part of Grámar, which declareth ý properties of words set alone one by one, without anye other joyned thereto. A *word* is a note whereby a thing is called. It is made of a sylla-

2   ble

ble. A *syllable* is a full oz perfect sound in a wozd : as foz example, Dos, flos : so likewise in dominus there are thzee syllables, do-mi-nus. A *syllable* is made of a Letter. A *letter* is a sound in a syllable which can not be devided : whose *prosodie* oz pzonuntiation is perceived by the po- wer : the *Orthographie* oz right wziting, by the fozme thereof. A *letter* is either a *vowell*, oz a *consonant*. A *vowell*, is a letter which maketh a sillable by it selfe. It is either *diducted* oz con- *tracted*. The *diducted vowell*, is pzonounced with open mouth, the tongue being with-dzawen to the pallate: as *a, e, i*. A soundeth most full with wide opening of the mouth, the tongue bending backe from the teeth to the roofe of the pallate, like the last sound, in ỹ Crows cry, as *Georg*: 1.

Tunc cornix plenam pluviã vocat improba voce,
Et sola in sicca secum spatiatur arena.

E, and *i*, are pzonounced with lesse opening of the mouth, the tongue beating against the pal- late of the under-teeth. *e* doth sound moze fully with a meane opening of the mouth, the tongue being fastened in the middle of the pallate, and upon the inner-most cheek-teeth: as in this ex- ample, *Æneid*. 2.

Degeneremã͡; Neoptolemum narrare memento.

i Soundeth moze straightly, as it were thzogh the teeth, with a lesser opening of the mouth, the tongue touching the uttermost of the pallat and the teeth next to the inner cheek-teeth : as foz example.

example. *Eclo.8.*

Credimus? an qui amant ipsi sibi somnia fingunt?

The contracted vowell is made, the mouth beeing drawne together, and the tongue put down
into the bottom of the mouth: as, *o,u,y.*

o Soundeth with a greater compasse, the tong
beeing drawen backe into the mouth: as for example. 2. *Æneid.*

ultrò Asiam magno Pelopeja ad mœnia bello.

V and *y*, are made with narrower compasse, the
tongue beeing something more drawne backe:
u, soundeth more basely with a meane compasse,
the middest of the tongue being bowed downe.
As for example. *Æneid.* 5.

unum pro multis dabitur caput.

y Doth sound with a smaller sound uppon the
neather lip, with the least compasse, the inner-
most part of the tongue beeing bowed downe: as
u the *liquid* doth in quis and sanguis.

A *consonant* is a letter which maketh a sound
onely with a *vowell*, and it is either a *semi-vowell*, or a *mute.*

A *semi-vowell* is that, which maketh a sound
like the halfe sound of a vowell. A *semi-vowell* is
either a *liquid*, or a *firme*. A *liquid* is pronounced
with open lips, like to the first sort of vowelles:
whose sound is sometimes more flat, and, as it
were, melteth in sounding: for which cause it is
called a *liquid* . But this *opening* is here *sharper,*
or more *flat: more flat*, as in *es, er* and *el.*

s, doth

s Doth hisse againste the teeth with a great
sound, the tongue beating againste the uttermost part of the palate: as for example.

Formosam resonare doces Amarillida sylvas:
Sic canibus catulos similes, sic matribus hædos.

This hissing beeing stronger in some Greeke
wordes, is written with the Greeke character,
Zeta: as in Zopyrus, Zephyrus: which z beeing
in the middest of a Greeke word, when it is varied in Latin, is rather expressed by a dubble *ss*,
as in this place of *Plautus* : Non Atticissat, sed
Sicelissat, for atticizei, Sicelizei.

R and *l* are pronounced, the lippes being lesse
opened.

r Doth hur with a meane sound, the tongue
beating the inner palate, and trembling about
the teeth: as for example.

Africa terribili tremit horrida terra tumultu.

l Soundeth with the least sound, the tongue
beating the rootes of the palate, yet more fully, in the end of a sillable, or beeing put after an
other consonant, and more gently, following it
selfe. In the beginning it is meane : as for example.

Sibila lambebant linguis - - - Also
- - *ubi mollis amaracus illum*
Floribus & dulci aspirans complectitur umbra.

The more flat opening is in *m*, and *n*.

m Doth humme within, the lippes being shut
fast at the utter part of the mouth, more fullye

in

in the beginning of the worde, more obscurelye in the ende, and meanely in the middest : as for example,

Tantæ molis erat Romanam condere gentem.

n Doth ring in the lips and the nose, the tong bending backe towarde the roofe of the palate, more sharpe in the beginning and the ende, but more flat in the middest: as for example.

Et lunam in nimbo nox intempesta tenebat,

And also *Æneid. 6.*

His Phædrā Procrinǵ, locis, mœstamǵ, Eriphylen.

But as concerning the five *liquids*, which in time past did melt, onely two, to wit, *r* and *l* did afterward remaine.

A firme *semi-vowell* is pronounced, the lippes being drawne togeather, like unto the seconde sort of vowells: and hath an immutable sounde, whereof it is called firme, as *jod, vau, ef.*

jod doth make a whizzing sound with a larger compasse, in the vtter part of the pallate and the teeth: as,

jam pater Æneas & jam Trojana juventus.

Vau and *ef* doe sound with a straight compasse.

v With a meane compasse, doth humme more baselye with the upper lippe : as in this example.

- - brevibusǵ, vadis frustraǵ, vocantem.

f Is blowne out more smoothly with the least compasse by the neather lip: as for example,

Forsitan & Priami fuerant quæ fata requiris.

A *mute* is a consonant, which alone doth onely mutter, as it were a certaine endeuour to pronounce : and it is either *open* or *shut* : open which doth mutter more softly, the lips being opened, partly in the teeth, and partlye in the pallate : in the teeth, as *te* and *de.*

t Doth sound more strongly, the tongue pressing the upper-teeth : as for example.

O Tite tute Tati tibi tanta tyranne tulisti.

o Soundeth more softlye, the tongue affecting the nether teeth more straightly, and the upper-teeth but a little : as,

Condebat donis opulentum & numine divæ.

Ce, Qu, and Ge, do mutter in the pallate.

c Doth sound more strongly, the tongue pressing the utter pallate and the inner cheek-teeth : as for example,

Quo res cunq₃ cadunt, unum & commune periclum.

k Is altogeather the same in sound with *c*, & utterly unusuall in Latine wordes.

q Doth follow *c* altogeather with the same sound, but is onely used before *u,* the *melting vowell,* when an other vowell followeth : as for example,

Nunc quo quanq₃ modo possis cognoscere, dicam.

g Soundeth more softly, the tongue pressing the middle of the pallate and the teeth next the inner cheeke-teeth : as for example.

Agno-

Agnovit longé genitum præsaga mali mens

In Cnæus and Cajus, *g* is pronounced for *c*. Here also there is a Greeke character in writing, called *Ix*, used for the two consonantes *Cs*, or *Gs*, as in crux and frux, which may be perceiued by the genitive case, crucis and frugis.

A *mute*, that is shutte, is that which doth mutter in the inner cheeke, the lips being shut, as *Be* and *Pe*.

b Is more straightly helde in: but *p*, with a more soft sounde, breaketh foorth through the middle of the lips: as,

Barbaricopostes auro spolijsque superbi.

Ha is a note of aspiration, which goeth before vowels alone, yet it followeth fowre consonants, and that onely in Greeke wordes: as for example. *Hamus, Herus, Hilum, Homo, Humus, Hydra, Rhodus, Thorus, Chorus, Phillis.*

And this is the distribution of Letters: whose kindes till now, haue beene disorderly and confusedly put together, and with certain compendiaries of writing, are thus numbred.

A, b, c, d, e, f, g, h, i, k, l, m, n, o, p, q, r, ſ, t, u, x, y, z. whereunto adde *j*, and *v*, and the number is 25.

Moreouer, in Letters there be greater, midle and final characters, which we use in the beginning of verses, periods, and proper names, and also in the midle and ende.

CAP.

CAP. 2.

Of the composition and quantity of sillables.

ANd thus farre concerning the true orthographie wryting, and pronunciation of a *letter*: which is either a *syllable* by it selfe, or part of a sillable. A *syllable* of one letter is every vowell: as *a,e,i,o,u*. A *syllable* of many letters is of vowels alone, or of a vowell and a consonaunt mixt togeather: that which is of *vowels alone*, is of two, & therefore is called a dipthongue, that is the sound of two vowels comprehended in one sillable, and that is foure-folde, *æ,au,œ,eu* : such are the firste syllables in *ætas, audio, œstrum, euge.*

A *sillable mixt of a vowell and a consonant*, maye contayne divers letters: sometimes two; as *ab*: sometimes three, as, ars : sometimes foure, as mars : sometimes five, as stans: sometimes six; where if three consonantes goe afore the vowell, onely two shall follow: or if two go afore, three shall follow, as in scrobs, stirps.

But the joyning togeather of continued consonants, as it is in the word, so it ought to be in the wryting, that those that are pronounced joyntly, ought to be written joyntly. This *Etymologie* doth chieflye appertaine to the middest of the simple worde : where consonantes are to be joyned togeather, which ought to be joyned

in the beginning of a worde : which for one to
devide by sillables,were barbarisme. Therfore
in Testis, omnis, magnus, aruspex, the last sillable is *stis,mnis,gnus,spex.*

Now the devision of a sillable in Latine
wordes (for it is otherwise in certaine Greeke
wordes)doth depend uppon a contrarye conjunction of consonants: for those which are not joyned,are devided. One rule is here common : If
in a simple worde of two sillables, the former
end in a consonant, the latter shall begin with a
consonant, and if the latter begin with a vowel,
the former shall end in a vowell: and if a simple
consonant be in the middest, it shall be referred
to the sillable that followeth : as in *Gallus, pi-*
us, pater: these are the sillables, *Gal-lus, pi-us,*
pa-ter.

A *sillable* is eyther short or long. A *short silla-*
ble is that, which doth consist of one time, and if
need be, it is noted over the vowell with this
marke (˘): & a *short sillable* is first a vowell comming before another, of the sillable following
in the same worde: as the first sillable in deus.
Yet in Greeke wordes the proper quantitie
must be observed, as in diûs. Secondly, *a,e,y,*in
the end of a word, as musa, lege, moly. Thirdly, every vowell before these letters, *r,l,s,t,d,m,b,*
in the end of a word: as jubar, nihil, legit, a-
pud, templum, ab. Fourthly, *i,*and *u,*before *s,*in
the end of a word, as tristis, bonus.

A long syllable is that which doth consist of two times, and that, if there bee any neede, is noted over the vowel with this mark: (-) *A syllable is long* either *by nature* or *by position.* Long by nature is first every dipthongue: as the first sillable in ætas, audio, cœna, euge: for each vowell hath one time at the least, & yet *u* being in the same syllable betweene, *q,* or *g,* and another vowell, doth melt away, and hath the sounde of the sixt Vowell, and then those two vowelles can not make a long syllable, as lingua, queror, quis, sanguis the like is to be saide when it commeth betweene, *s,* & *a,* or *s,* & *e,* as *suadeo, suavis, consuesco, consuetus.* Secondly long by nature is *i,* and *u,* in the ende of a worde, as in veni, and manu. Thirdly, every vowell before, *n,* and *c,* in the end of a word, as Titan, splen, delphin, Xenophon, Phorcyn (but no Latine word doth end in *un*) illac, halec, dic, hoc, duc. Fourthly, *a, e, o,* before *s,* in the end of a worde: as amas, potes, nepos.

A long syllable by position is, when two *consonantes* doe followe the vowell of a syllable in the same word: as ast, pax, gaza, Maja, ajo Pompejus. For there is a double compendious note in writing, used for two simple notes severed: and *i,* in the middle of two vowels of the same simple word is long as well as *x,* and *z.* Also *the sillable is long by position,* when of two consonants one is in the end of the worde going before, foze, the other in the beginning of the word following; as,

--- *Deus nobis hæc otia fecit.*

Except when the liquid, *r* or *l*, in the same syllable follow any of these seven Consonants, *f, t, d, c, g, b, p,* comming after a vowell that is short by nature: for then they melt away, and therefore make a doubtfull syllable: as Afri, arbitror, exedra, volucris, demigro, celebris, apros, Atlas, abodlas, Agathocles, Noegla, Hibla, locuples, ciniflo.

o In the end of a worde is common: as *homo, amo:* yet in wordes of one syllable it is long, as *ô, sto, flo, do, pro:* but in true writing of the quantity, the greatest difference is in doubful words, as malus, for *a Tree,* and malus, that is, *not good,* which are to be distinguished by their marke, if ambiguity be feared.

Cap. 3.

Of Accent and Notation.

THus farre concerning the parts of a *worde.* The common affections of a word are *Accent* and *Notation.* An *accent* is that, whereby the word is as it were tuned, and there is but one *accent* in a worde, although there bee many syllables, and it is *sharp, or flat.* By the *sharp* Accent a syllable is lifted up. The *flat* Accent is

either

eyther *grave* o2 *bended* : by the *grave accent* the
fillable is depzeſſed: by the *bended* it is both lifted up and alſo depzeſſed . So now they all, if
there be anye need, are noted thus : the *ſharpe* a,
the *grave* à, the *bended* â.

The *ſharpe accent* onely hath beene of long
time uſed, o2 rather a certaine *pauſe* fo2 everye
accent, which *pauſe* maye bee called an *accent*.
Therefoze in all wozdes of one fillable, the *accent* is well knowne in ſum, es, eſt : in woꝛdes
of two fillables the laſt but one hath the *accent*,
as in bonus, rarus : but in woꝛdes of many fillables the laſt but one being long, eyther by nature, as Romanus; o2 by poſition, and yet not
doubtfull, as Seneſco. Jf it be ſhoꝛt o2 doubtful,
the *accent* ſhall be in the laſt ſaving two, as dominus, celebris, volucris : but in a verſe the *accent* doth follow the law of the verſe ; as foꝛ example,

Pecudes pictæ̃q̃, volucres.

An *interrogation* doth chaunge the *accent*, and
doth remove it unto the laſt fillable: as *Teren.
Eun.* ſed quid ego ? Likewiſe a note to diſtin-
guiſh : as in *una, verò*, and in other doubtfull
woꝛdes, in pronouncing and wꝛiting whereof
this ſhall be the diſtinction.

Notation is that whereby the *kinde* o2 *figure*
of ỹ woꝛd is ſought out. The *kinde* is the *notation*, whereby is ſought out, whether the woꝛde
be the pꝛimitive of that kinde, o2 derived of
some

some other primitives: the primitive, as *ame*, that which is derived of it, is *amabilis*.

Sometimes the *kinde* doth change the quantitie of wordes : as the first sillable in *Luceo* is long, in *lateo* it is short, but it is otherwise in *Lucerna* and *Laterna*; as for example,

Dux laterna viæ clausis feror aurea flammis,
Et tuta est gremio parva lucerna meo.

So of Igni is made igniculus, of navi navicula, and such like. *Figure* is that, whereby we seeke whether the word be *simple*, or *compounded*: Simple; as doctus, amo: Compounded, as perdoctus, redamo. This composition doth sometimes chaunge the letters, as Cognosco for connosco. It doth also chaunge the joyning of the consonants, and likewise the division of thé: as in Abutor, inaccessus, the first sillable endeth in a consonant : and that following beginneth with a vowell: so abstemius (because the word is compounded of abs, and temeto) shall leave, *s*, a letter of the first sillable to the next. *Composition* doth also sometimes alter the quantitie of sillables; as omni, and cuncti, and such like, do make the laste sillable long, which is made short in omnipotens, and cunctipotens.

Cap. 4.

Of the genders of a Noune.

B

A Word is either of *Number*, or *without number*. A word of number is that, which over and beside the proper signification, doth signifie some number, and that eyther *singular* or *plurall*. Whereupon a *word of number* is called *singular*, or *plurall*. The * *singular number* is that, whereby a singular thing may bee expressed; as *Doctus, Legit*. *The plurall*, whereby many thinges may be expressed; as *Docti, Legunt*. A word of number is varied by certaine endes, whereupon the worde is called *finite*, which in some certain end of variation doth signifie a definite number, beside the proper signification, as *Doctus, legit*. An *infinite* word, noteth not anye certaine number besides his proper signification, as nequam, præsto, amare, amandi.

A *word of number*, is eyther a *noune* or a *Verbe*. A *noune* is a word of number that hath *gender* and *case*. The *gender* is a difference of a *noune* according to the *sexe*, and is eyther *simple* or *manifold*: that which is *simple*, is eyther *naturall*, or *feined*: the *naturall* is eyther ȳ *Masculine* or *feminine*. A *noune* of the *Masculine Gender* is that before which this *Pronoune hic* may be placed: of which sort, are all things which doe agree to the male-kinde, or to those things which are conceived by the malekinde: as Marcus, Catelina, Dinacium, Pistor, Architectus, Nauta, Bonus, Doctus, Neptunús, Lucifer. Boreas, Sequana, Aprilis.

A *Noune of the feminine Gender* is that, before which

*The moste proper names, and some names of corne, hearbes, liquors and metals, haue this number onely. *Some proper names are of this number only: as Thebæ, Athenę, &c.

which this Pronoune hæc may be put: of which
kinde are Nounes agreeing to the female, or
thinges conceiued by the female-kinde: as Tul
lia, Glycerium, Pallas, obſtetrix, docta, bona.
Also names of countries, * Cities and trees are
of the feminine gender. The names of countries, as *Ægyptus, Samos* : of Cities, as *Roma,
Carthago, Lacedæmon* : of trees, as *Ceraſus pyrus*
are alſo of the feminine gender.

But ſometimes the Maſculine and feminine
genders are doubtfull: and the ſame worde doth
agree to both ſexes: as Aquila both for male &
female, is of the feminine gender : and paſſer of
the maſculine gender. But to diſcerne the ſexe
we ſay, aquila mas, aquila fæmina. A noune of
the feined gender is that, before the which this
article hoc may be put, and it is called the neuter: as hoc templum. A ſpecial noune doth ſom-
times follow the gender of a generall noune: as
Eunuchus is of the maſculine gender: *Terence*
ſayth, Tranſtulit in Eunuchum ſuam: for fabula is here underſtood. Albula, becauſe it is a ri-
ver, is of the maſculine gender. Yet *Ovid. 4.
Faſt.* ſayth, Albula pota deo. Where aqua is
underſtood.

That gender which is manifold, is either cōmon, or of every gender. That is a noune of the
common gender, before which may be put, hic
& hæc: as civis, ſacerdos, homo: as homo nata erat. Nec vox hominem ſonat, ſayth *Maro*

* There ar
manye ex-
ceptions
from this
rule, which
follow in
their orde

F   of

of a woman. A noune of everye gender is that, before which may be put both hic and hæc and hoc: as fælix, amans.

And by the difference of the gender, the noune is eyther a *substantive* or *Adjective*. A *substantive* is a noune of a simple gender, or at the most of a duble gender. A *substantive* being of one gender, & a proper name, is noted with a great letter: as *Maro, Horatius*. An *Adjective* is a Noune of three genders, eyther in one ende, as fælix, amans, and also wordes infinite, as ejusmodi, istjusmodi, illjusmodi, hujusmodi, damnas, mancipi, præsto, frugi: or in two · as fortis forte: or in three ends, as bonus, bona, bonum: acer, acris, acre: sequester, sequestris, sequestre: equester, equestris, equestre.

CAP. 5.

Of the comparison of Adjectives.

+Increase of ignifications.

*C Omparison doth happen unto moste *Adjectives*, as cōtrarywise *diminution* doth unto substantives. There are two degrees of comparison after the *absolute* : the *comparative* and the *superlative*. The *comparative* is that, which is expressed by the *absolute*, with this Adverbe magis: as doctior, magis doctus. The *superlative*, which is expressed by the *absolute*, with this Adverb maximè: as doctissimus, maxime doctus. Both degrees are formed of the *absolute* ending

ending in *i*: the *comparative* by adding *or* fo2 the
common gender, and *us* fo2 the neuter as of do-
ɛ̄i,doctior, doctius: forti,tortior,fortius:ira-
ti,iratior, iratius:preclari, præclarior, præcla-
rius. The Superlative by adding *ſſimus* fo2 the
maſculine,ꝗ *ſſima* fo2 the feminine, *ſſimum* fo2 y̓
neuter:as Doctiſsimus , doctiſsima, doctiſsi-
mum:Fortiſsimus,fortiſsima,fortiſsimum:ſo
Iratiſsimus,præclariſsimus.Jf the *abſolute* end
in *er*,the ſuperlative of y̓ maſculine ſhal be made
by putting to *rimus*,the feminine *rima*,the neuter *rimum*,as niger, nigerrimus,nigerrima,ni-
gerrimum . But fo2 the moſt part of the th2ee
degrees,one is wanting, an other is fo2med out
of rule,as may be ſeene by thoſe that follow:ex-
terior,extremus ꝗ extimus: interior,intimus:
inferior,inſimus:ocyor, ocyſsimus: ulterior,
ultimus:ſuperior,ſupremus: deterior,deteri-
mus: citerior,citimus: poſterior, poſtremus :
propior,proximus(wherof ariſeth a new comparative,proximior)prior,primus:adoleſcens
adoleſcentior:ingens, ingentior:infinitus,in-
finitior:ſatur, ſaturior:ſenex,ſenior: juvenis,
iunior:dives,divitior:ſiniſter, ſiniſterior, ſini-
ſtimus:ſacer, magis ſacer,ſacerimus:vetus,ve-
terior,veterrimus:frugi, frugalior, frugaliſsi-
mus:maturus,maturior,maturiſsimus ꝗ ma-
turrimus : malus, peior, peſsimus : magnus,
maior,maximus : multus, plus, fo2 the Neuter of the ſingular number onelye, plurimus:

nequam,

Nequam, nequior, nequissimus : dexter, dexterior, dextimus. Novissimus fo2 the last, is the onely degree. Bonus, melior, optimus. Parvus, minor, minimus, and parvissimus, in Lucretius. Maledicus, maledicentior, maledicentissimus : magnificus, magnificentior, magnificentissimus : benevolus, benevolentior, benevolentissimus, and such like. Five wo2des in *lis*, make *limus* in the Superlative; as Agilis, agilior, agillimus: Humilis, humilior, humillimus: Similis, similior, simillimus: Facilis, facilior, facillimus: gracilis, gracilior, gracillimus.

Adjectives ending in *us* pure, are not compared: as Aureus, pius: (though Curtius useth pijssimus, but *Cicero* doth not allow of it: yet tenuior, tenuissimus: and we saye assiduissimé: & vlpian hath idoneior of idoneus) in *dus*, as colendus: in *imus*, as optimus: in *plex*, as multiplex: (*Quintilian* useth simplicius) in *ivus*, as deliberativus (yet we read festivior, and festivissimus) in *tinus* as matutinus: wo2des derived of fero and gero, as legifer, armiger and manye others, as equester, silvester, degener, memor, cicur, vulgaris, Gallicus, vetulus.

CAP. 6
Of Diminution.

A *Diminutive* is a Noune without comparison, signifying in the same kinde the *Diminution*, of his P2imative. And doth end in *io*, *us*, er. Io, as of Ardea, ardelio: of homo, homuncio: of senex, senecio.

Eus, as of equus, equuleus: but hæc acus maketh aculeus: these two ends are moze rare. but lus doth containe a great nûber of diminutives, l, beeing sometimes single, somtimes duble: the endes of single l, are, olus, and ulus, and culus, the last sillable but one being shozt.

Olus, ola, olû, is made of som case ending in o, as of filio, filiolus: so tulliolus, alveolus, capreolus: filia, Tullia, filiola, Tulliola: also neuters, negotiolû, palliolum: yet of homo, homulus.

ulus Doth chaunge s, of the Nominative case into lus: as servus, servulus, gracus, graculus: so tantulus, parvulus; vetus, vetulus, vetula; paulus, paululus: of rege commeth regulus (but adolescens hath adolescentulus) Like-wise feminines, lunula, animula, aquula, sylvula, mensula, literula, furcula: caput capitulum. Culus hath very many whereof the most part do onely adde culus and culum, as in wozdes of one sillable, flos, flosculus: so masculus, musculus: of cor, corculum: so neuters in us: as rus, rusculû: crus, crusculum: also of many sillables: munusculum, corpusculum, opusculum. So of lepus lepusculus. So of neuters comparatives there are Adjectives, Majusculus, majuscula, majusculum: so grandiusculus, minusculus, celeriusculus: so also of er, and or: as frater, fraterculus: paterculus: also pauperculus, paupercula, pau-

perculum: muliercula, matercula (notwithstã-
ding of venter, ventriculus) amator, amator-
culus: sororcula : but of rumor, rumusculus.
Certaine notwithstanding doe chaunge *o*, into
un: as homo, homunculus: so latrunculus: ty-
runculus: carbunculus, (and of Fur, furuncu-
lus) also feminines, offensio, offensiuncula, ra-
tiuncula : virguncula: some are formed by turning *is* in ÿ end into *culus*, as those which end in
x: dicax, dicacis, dicaculus: of facis, facula: fornacis, fornacula: cervicis, cervicula : some are
derived of the end in *i*, by shortning the last sillable therof, as those which end in *is*, *rs*, *ns*: as of
Ignis, igni, igniculus: so dulciculus : also feminines : as apicula, navicula, notwithstanding
iuvenal doth make *cuticula* long.

Cum bibet æstivum incontracta cuticula solem.
So of *Canis*, *Canicula*: Pers. *Insana Canicula mes-*
ses Vrit.

Rs, as pars, parti, particula, *ns*, as fons, fonti,
fonticulus: so monticulus, ponticulus: so lens,
lenti, lenticula. A word ending in *ui*, looseth *u*,
as of artui, articulus: so versiculus: but hoc cur-
riculum: as geniculum, corniculum : domus,
domuncula.

Some do forme the end in *e*, and do make that
e, long, as those which ende in *es*: so of res commeth recula: of vulpes, vulpecula: so nubecula,
diecula: but yet of merces commeth mercedu-
la. And thus much of single *l*.

llus, *l* Being duble is made first of *nus*, *na*, *num*:

then of *er,ra,rum:lus,la,lum* : *nus*, as Asinus, asi-
na: asellus, asella: so gemellus, gemella, gemel-
lum: so of bonus, bellus, bella, bellum: agnus,
agnellus: pugnus, pugillus: unus, ullus: vinum,
villum: catena, catella: columna, columella, &
columnella: tignum, tigillum: so signum, sigil-
lum, but of scamnum commeth scabellum : of
scutum, commeth scutella: of rana, ranunculus:
so of anguis, anguilla.

Er, as of Ager, agellus: liber, libellus: tenel-
lus, cultellus : of puer, puellus & puella : so li-
bella, umbella: sacrum, sacellum: so lucrum, lu-
cellum flabrum, flabellum.

Lus,la,lum: as populus, popellus: catulus, ca-
tellus: paululus, pauxillus: of homulus, homú-
culus: codex, codiculus, codicillus : fabula, fa-
bella: tabula, tabella: velum, vexillum: tantu-
lum, tantillum. Therfore *l*, going before, there
is great plenty of *diminutives*.

Ter. This latter end is more seldome, as Surdaster, Antoniaster with *Cicero*, and Parasitaster with *Terence*. Also certaine Greeke wordes
are usurped in Latin, as Syriscus, with *Terence*.
And many have but only a shew of *diminutives*:
as Cuniculus, tabula, periculum . And thus
much of *genders of Nounes*, and of *Comparisons*,
and *Diminutions*.

Cap. 7.
Of Case, and the first Declination being
of even sillables.

Case

CAse is the speciall ending of a Noune, & is sixefolde: the *Nominative*, the *Genitive*, the *Dative*, the *Accusative*, the *Vocative*, & the *Ablative*. There are two Cases a like; the Nominative & the vocative, in both numbers: the dative, & the Ablative, in the plurall: as, magister, magister, magistri, magistri: also magistris, magistris. And in Nounes of the neuter gender, these cases are like in both numbers, the Nominative, the Accusative, and the Vocative, & in the plurall they ende all in *a*: as Templum, templa: tempus, tempora.

The varying of a noune according to the case is called *Declination*. *Declination* is eyther of even, or of uneven syllables. The Declination of even sillables is, where the Dative plurall ending in *is*, is of even sillables with the Nominative singular: as musa, musis, dominus, dominis, and that is double. The first, which in the Nominative case singular doth ende in *a* feminine, in the Genitive in *a*, in the Dative in *a*, in the Accusative in *am*, in the Ablative in *a*: in the Nominative case plurall in *e*, in the Genitive in *arum*, in the Accusative in *as*: as, Musa, musae, musae, musam, musa, musa: musae, musarum, musis, musas, musae, musis. So Bura, amicitia, inimicitia, arena, rosa, ruta, myrica, faba, cepa, genista.

Masculines in *as*, or *es*, and proper names of the feminine gender in *e*, being Greeke wordes
of

of the first declination of even sillables, do here
keepe oft times the Greeke end: as Æneas, Æ-
neæ,Æneæ:Sophistes,sophistæ,sophiste:Hele-
ne,Helenes,Helenæ: Anchises, Anchisæ, An-
chisæ:Penelope,Penelopes,Penelope . For in
Appellatiues , which end in *es* , the Latinistes
haue more comonly retained the Latine forme:
as, Ænea,sophista,Helena, grammatica,rhe-
torica,logica,poetica, geometra, bibliopola.

Wordes noting parētage or kindred, ending
in *es*,of the masculine , & *e*,of the feminine gender, are all of this declination: as *Priamides* , he
which is of the stocke of *Priamus* : and *Nerine*,
which is come of the stocke of *Nereus*.

The *anomaly* of number. Nounes that are seldome used in one of the numbers, as in the plu-
rall:eloquentia,sapientia, & such like substantiues: also adorea,fama,fuga,cholera,gloria. *
And these folowing are seldome used in the singular number:argutiæ, antiæ, aquæ,calidæ,e-
pulæ,exequiæ, exuviæ, excubiæ, insidiæ, inferiæ, induciæ, salinæ, scalæ,deliciæ , manubiæ,
minæ,nugæ,nuptiæ,valvæ,salæ,facetiæ, feriæ,
thermæ,tenebræ, divitiæ, calendæ, cunæ,cli-
tellæ,quisquiliæ,balenæ,bigæ,quadrigæ, Pha-
leræ. Some nounes are declined fullie in both
numbers , but yet in a diuerse signification : as
Apina and Trica,the names of townes: apinæ,
tricæ,for trifels:scopa a kinde of viole,and sco-
pæ,a dragnet:although Columella hath scopu-
la:

* Desidia, senecta,stul-titia, invi-dia.&c.

* Inferiæ, plagæ.

la:litera a letter, & literæ, an Epistle. Nundina
a Goddesse, & nūdinæ for faires, which returne
euery ninth day, fidicula, a small instrument, fi-
diculæ wherewith those which are giltie are
tormeted:dira, of dirus, dira, dirum, cruell Di-
ræ, Furies : so in Nounes that signifie number,
prima, secunda, nona, decima, & plurally, pri-
mæ, secūdæ, nonæ, decimæ: primitiæ, the adiectiue being primitius, primitia, primitium , &
many other such like. Dica, dicā, dica, is a word
of three cases, & Dicis , after the Greeke forme:
as Dicis causa, Suppetiæ, suppetias: repetun-
darum, repetundis, a word of two cases: infici-
as, a word of one case.

The *Anomalie* of case. Here is one genitiue
case of the Greeke forme in the Latine noune
familias, & in the compoundes, pater-familias,
mater-familias, filius-familias:so patres , ma-
tres, filii-familias:yet familiæ, and familiarum
are used.

The accusatiue of Greeke words that end in
as, hath more commonly *n*, then *m* : of wordes in
es and *e*, *n* onely: as Æneas , Ænean : Anchises, Anchisen, Penelope, Penelopen.

The vocatiue doth cast away, *s*, when the nominatiue endeth in *as*, or *es* : as Ænea , Anchise.

If the nominatiue end in *es* or in *e* : the ablatiue shall end in *e*: as Anchise, Penelope.

The genitiue case of the plurall number is
here

here contracted sometimes by the Poetes, & is thus noted â. 3, Æneid. Graiugenûmque domus. Lucretius. 1. Æneadûm genitrix.

The Datiue and the Ablatiue in sir substantiues doth make abus, as equabus, libertabus, filiabus, mulabus, natabus, deabus. Yet notwithstanding equis, natis and filijs, are used, if the ambiguitie of the sere be distinguished. Scævola in the Prædian law sayd, conservabus.

*The *Anomalie* of the gender. Adria is of the masculine gender: so cometa, Planeta, & others of the first Greeke declinatiõ: Margarita, charta, chataracta, catapulta, cochlea, gausapa, are excepted, which are masculines in the Greeke.

*So is, scurra, rabula, assecla, scriba, lixa, lanista.

These are counted of the cõmon gender, Verna, conviva, and compoundes of venio, colo, & gigno: as advena, convena, agricola, cœlicola, indigena, terrigena.

Auriga.

CAP. 8.
Of the second declination of even syllables.

THe second declination of even syllables, is that, which in ẙ nominatiue case singular endeth in these letters, s, or r, masculine, or in *m* neuter: in the genitiue in *i*, in the datiue and the ablatiue in o, in the accusatiue in *m*, in the nominatiue case plurall in *i* or *a*: in the genitiue in *orum*, in the accusatiue in *os*, or *a*.

The Greeke case doth sometimes remaine

as

as Samos,Lesbos,for Samus & Lesbus : Ilion,
for Iliũ,Pergamon for Pergamum, Androgeo
for Androgei,Orphei for Orpheo,Ilionea for
Ilioneum,Theseu for Thesee, Panthou for Pã-
thoê:Cimmerion for Cimmeriorum.

The genitive singular , having i doubled, is
sometimes abridged by the poetes. Iuvenal.

Antoni' gladios potuit contemnere.---
Virg. 1.Eclog.

Nec spes libertatis erat,nec cura peculi.

But the plural in prose,is oftentimes contra-
cted:as, Deûm, fabrûm, procûm, sestertiûm,
virûm,for Deorum,fabrorum, procorum, se-
stertiorum , virorum.

s, As Dominus,domini, domino, dominũ,
domine,domino. Domini,dominorũ, dominis,dominos,domini, dominis. In like manner Gallus,Hyacinthus,Lupinus,crocus,por-
rus:also maledicus, causidicus,pronubus.

, Vesperus ,
vesper.

These nounes that follow do want the plurall
number : humus,viscus, fimus , limus, cestus,
bolus,pontus: Contrariwise,these that follow
want the singular number:as Inferi,superi,Li-

● Gabii,lo-
ri.

beri,Ludi,fasti,fori,cani,cancelli,posteri. Macte, macti , is a word of two cases among the
grammarians.

us In the nominative, is turned into *e* in the
vocative:but three do end in *i:*as filius,fili, meus,mi:genius,geni: Deus doth remaine in the
vocative case:also *us* is také away from proper
names

names that end in *ius*,the *accent* being brought
backe into the last syllable but two: as Antonius,Antoni: and those which in the nominatiue
case haue j,lose *us* in the vocatiue, and the consonant is turned into the vowel *i*, the quantitie
of the vowel going before,being kept: as Cajus
Caj.Pompejus,Pompei.

The nominatiue case plural of this word Deus is usual,dii or di· wherof cōmeth diis or dis.

The *gender*. These nounes are of the masculine gender,though they be the names of trees:
to wit,spinus,rubus,libanus:cōtrariwise these
that follow are of the feminine gender, alvus
vannus,humus:ficus for a tree,& the fruit: but
morbus is of the masculine geder: also domus
is of the feminine gender, hauing in the genitiue case singular domi, in the accusatiue domum, it wanteth the vocatiue,& hath domo in
the ablatiue:& in the plural number it hath do-
morū,domos,Abydos & Lesbos , though they
be names of townes, are used of Poetes in the
masculine gender.Greeke nounes of this declination for the most part,are of the feminine gēder. as Lecythus, nardus, crystallus, balanus,
papyrus:but these are of the cōmon gender,co-
lus,grossus,phaselus,pharus, pāpinus, penus
without the plurall nūber. *Cicero* thinketh this
word atomus to be of the feminine gender,and
Seneca of the masculine: vulgus wanteth the
plural number,and is of the masculine & neuter
gender:

*Antidotus
costus, diph
tongus,bys-
sus,synodus,
&c.
Paradisus.

gender: Pelagus and virus are of the neuter gēder, and want the plurall number.

Some nounes of this secōd declination of evē
syllables do end in *er*: as Magister, magistri, ma
gistro, magistrū, magister, magistro: magistri,
magistrorum, magistris, magistros, magistri,
magistris. So likewise oleaster is declined.

These increase in the genitive case, having
the last syllable save one short: as Armiger, Ar-
migeri: signifer, signiferi, and others derived
of fero, and gero: so asper, exter, liber, miser,
tener, dexter, gibber, prosper: and these substantives, adulter, socer, gener, puer: but Iber,
Iberi: and hereof Celtiber, Celtiberi, yet Pro-
sperus, and Iberus, as yet are perfect. *Cato* u-
seth cæterus: as cæterus ornatus: also puerus
hath bene in use.

These nounes following do likewise increase
as vir, viri, and the compoundes thereof, leuir,
triumvir, decemvir, and such like: also satur,
saturi.

Nounes in *m*, as scamnum, scamni, scamno,
scamnum, scamnū, scamno: scamna, scamno-
rū, scamnis, scamna, scamna, scamnis. So cal-
lum, connubium: So gausapū, hordeum, ele-
ctrum, lilium, lolium, mustum, mulsum, vinū,
viburnum, defrutum, cinnamomum, or cin-
namum, balsamum, pisum: so jugerum.

These nounes following want the plurall nūber,* aurum, argentum, acetum, apiū, ervum,
epulum,

Senium,
aratrum,
virus, vitrum

epulum,salum,sevum,oʒ sepum, oʒ sebum, sinum, stannum, lethum, hilum , nihilum, ni-
trum,justitium,viscum,fœnum,tabum, triti-
cum,delicium,cœlum,cœnum,garum, gluti-
num,butyrum,penum: tātundem tantidem,
a woʒd of two cases ✝ Contrarywise these that
follow,want the singular number:ˮ arma, effa-
ta,exta,sata,munia,iusta,vasa,vinacea, flabra,
fraga , tesqua , comitia , cibaria, (yet comiti-
um , foʒ the place , is of both numbers) cibaria cnnabula , crepundia , bellaria , præcordia,parapherna✝

    The gēder. Nounes that end in *um* are whol-
ly of the neuter gender (if they be not the pʒoper names of men oʒ women) although they be
the names of countries: as Illiricum,Noricum
oʒ of Cities: as Avaricum, Brundusium: oʒ of
trees,as Cinnamomum,balsamum✝

    These nounes that follow do change their gē-
der with their termination: Avernus, Ismarus,
Mænalus,Massicus,Tænarus,Taygetus , Din-
dymus, Pangæus,tartarus, sibilus,carbasus a
woʒd of the feminine gender.And in the plurall
number they are neuters : as Averna , Ismara,
Mænala,Massica,Tænara,Taygeta,Dindyma,
Pangea, tartara, sibila,carbasa : but E!ysium,
Rastrum, frenum,have in the plurall number
Elisii , rastri , freni, and sometimes also frena:
but Argi is onely in the plurall number of the
masculine gender.

              Moʒe꞊

*Mænia,lu-
stra, mapa-
palia, castra,
sponsalia, ro
stra.&c.

Moreouer, some nounes are of two sortes making both *us* & *um*: as intubus, supparus, jugu-
lus, viscus, fimus, dupondius, chirographus,
(*Quintilian* hath cōmentarius) crocus, balteus
clypeus, baculus, porrus, pileus: intubū, suppa-
rū, jugulū, viscū, fimum, dupódium: chirogra-
phum, & *Cicero* hath commentarium: crocum,
clypeum, balteum, baculum, porrum, pileum.
Pergamus, & Pergamum hath onely in the plurall number Pergama: locus & jocus in the singular onely, but in the plurall number loci and
loca, joci and joca, and many other nounes of
this sort, which are not of one declinatiō alone,
but of diverse: as ganea and ganeum: *Ouid* hath
menda, and *Cicero* mendum: also amygdala &
amygdalum, for the fruite.

* Sinus and
sinum even-
tus & even-
tum. &c.

CAP. 9.

Of adjectives that be of evē syllables &
irregular, which are called Pronounes.

ADjectives of even syllables are of both de-
clinatiōs, but of a diverse gender: as bonus,
bona, bonum. Among adjectives of even sillables, are those which are commonly called *Pronounes*, wherof three, ego, tui, sui, are farthest out
of rule and have the last *i*, of the dative case singular, doubtfull. Ego, mei vel mis, mihi vel,
mi, me, me: Nos, nostrum vel nostri, nobis,
nos, nobis, here ech number is said to want the
voca-

vocatiue case.

Tu,tui o2 tis,tibi,te,tu, te:Vos, vestrū o2 vestri,vobis,vos,vos,vobis.Sui,sibi,se,se:Sui,si-
bi,se,se.This third p2onoune doth want the nominatiue & the vocatiue case of both numbers,
& these genitiues, mei,tui,sui, nostri , & vestri,
be used passiuely.Of these th2ee do arise fiue regular wo2des,meus,mea,meū· noster, nostra,
nostrum:tuus, tua,tuū· vester:vestra,vestrū,su
us,sua,suū·The rest of the adiectiues that be of
euen sillables , & irregular do mo2e apparantly
keepe ŷ cases of the first & second declination of
euē sillables.These sixtene folowing haue their
genitiues ending in us, & their datiues in i· but
the th2ee first haue their genitiues in ius,as hic,
hæc , hoc, hujus , huic (which sometimes is a
wo2d of one sillable)hunc,hanc, hoc hoc,hac,
hoc:in the plurall number hi,hæ,hæc, horum,
harum,horum:his:hos,has,hæc,his,Is,ea,id:
eius:ei:eū,eā,id:eo,ea,eo : ei o2 ij, sometimes
also i, eæ,ea:eorum, earum, eorum:eis o2 ijs,
sometimes also îs:eos:eas,ea:eis o2 ijs,& sometimes îs.Idem,eadem , idem,the compound is
declined after the same so2t.

Quis o2 qui,quæ o2 qua,quod o2 quid:cujus
cui,the last being doubtfull,& sometimes but of
one sillable:quē,quā, quod o2 quid:quo, qua,
quo,& sometimes qui,in euery gēder.Qui,quæ
quē,o2 qua:quorum,quarū,quorū:quibus, o2
quîs:quos,quas,quæ,o2 qua:quibus o2 quîs.

Quis is an interrogative oʒ an infinitive: qui
& quæ a relative,& somtimes alſo an interrogative,as 2.Philip.qui inde reditus.Quid is taken ſubſtantively , & quod adjectiuely. Qui is
cōpounded 4.wayes,as quilibet, quicūq;,qui-
dam quivis ; & quis in compoſition voth ſometimes go befoʒe:as in quiſquis,quiſq;,quiſquā
quiſnam,quiſpiā,and in all thoſe that went befoʒe, ẙ feminine voth onely end in *æ*:as neuters
of ẙ plural nūber :as quælibet,quæcunq; quædam,quævis,quæq;,quæquam,quænam,quæ-
piā:yet quiſquis,quicquid,quoquo,be onely ẙ
caſes that are in uſe : but quæquam and quod-
quā are rare. Sometimes Quis voth follow,as
aliquis,ecquis,ſiquis, nequis,nūquis . Theſe
feminines vo onely end in *a*,as the plurall neu-
ters:as aliqua,ecqua,ſiqua,nequa,nunqua.

   Theſe thirtene *adjectives* that follow, in the
genitive caſe vo end in *ius* with *i* long: as Alius
alia aliud : alius:alii:iſte, iſta,iſtud:iſtius:iſti:
ille:illa,illud:illius:illi : ipſe,ipſa, ipſum , ipſi-
us : ipſi:unus,una,unum,and thoſe which are
verived hereof:ullus ulla, ullū:uter,utra, utrū:
& the compoundes of it : as uterque, utraque,
utrumque : neuter , neutra, neutrum:ſolus,
ſola,ſolum:totus, tota. totum : alter, altera,
alterum, maketh alterius, with *i* ſhoʒt:Of the
whole number of theſe thirtene , there be thʒee
which have ſix caſes,to wit,unus,ſolus,totus:
but ullus, nullus, alius, as Grammarians ſay,
DO

do want the vocatibe case. In these thirtene the genitibe and the datibe cases in tyme have ben regulare, and the Poetes do sometimes make the last sillable save one of the genitibe case, short. This compound alteruter, alterutra, alterutrum, is declined chiefly in the latter part of it alterutrius: of these sixtene, eight following, alius, alter, is, hic, iste, ille, ipse, qui, are relatives, having relation to some thing that went before: wherof hic, ille, iste, are demonstratives. Sui and suus, have a respect backe againe to the next antecedent, as 4. Fin.

Omnis natura est conservatrix sui.

The two that remain, Ambo, & duo, are thus declined, ambo, ambæ, ambo: amborū, ambarū amborū: ambob°, ambab°, ambobus: ambos, ambas, ambo: ambo, ambæ, ambo: ambobus, ambabus, ambobus. Duo, duæ, duo: duorū, duarū, duorū: duobus, duabus, duobus: duos, duas, duo: duo, duæ, duo: duobus, duabus, duobus. you shal sometimes read ambo, & duo, for ambos, and duos, & thus much of the declination which is of even sillables.

Cap. 10.

Of the first declination of uneven sillables.

The *declination of uneven sillables* is that, whose datibe case plural is of uneven sillables

2   bles

bles with the nominative singular, & it endeth
in the genitive case singular in *is*, in the dative
in *i*, in the accusative in *em*, or in the end of the
neuter, in the ablative in *e* : in the nominative &
accusative plurall in *es*, or in *a*, in the genitive in
um, in the dative & ablative in *ibus*. In this declination the Greeke case doth sometimes remaine, as in the accusative Parin, Pallada, and
without *s* in the vocative, Pari, Palla. The declination of uneven sillables is two-fold : the first
whose genitive case singular doth not increase,
& doth end in *e*, *us*, or *r*, in the nominative case.

Those which do end in *e*, *is*, are of the neuter
gender: as, mantile, mantilis, mantili, mantile,
mantile, mantili: mantilia, mantilia, mantiliũ, mantili-
bus, mantilia, mantilia, mātilibus: so lacte, lactis, a word out of use, and wanting the plurall
number: whereof lac, lactis is contracted: lactes:
lactiũ, lactibus, of the feminine gender, & wanting the singular number : this word mille being a substantive hath but one case in the singular number, & in the plurall it is declined fully;
but when it is an adjective, it is declined in the
plurall number onely, and that but in one case.
Also conclaue, Præneste, & adjectiues ending in
e, as dulce, triste, and such like are neuters: so is
the word of one case, Cære.

The ablative case doth alwayes end in *i*, even
in adjectiues: as, Tristis, triste, tristi: acer, acris,
acre, acri, and such like.

The

The nominative case plurall in *ia*, as aplustria, which is also contracted aplustra. These nounes following do want the singular nũber: altaria, magalia, mapalia : also Agonalia, Bacchanalia, Saturnalia, and such like names of festivall dayes : also sponsalia.

The genitive case plurall in the names of festivall dayes, is of the second declination of even sillables, as Agonalium, Agonaliorum, Saturnalium, Saturnaliorum. Bacchanalium, Bacchanaliorum: which hath bene used in certaine others, as Anciliorum for Ancilium : so Sponsaliorum for Sponsalium : Vectigaliorum for vectigalium.

These which end in *s*, are of the feminine gẽder, and end in *es* or *is*, and in the genitive case plurall in *ium*.

Es,is: as vulpes, vulpis, vulpi, vulpem, vulpes, vulpe: vulpes, vulpiũ, vulpibus, vulpes, vulpes, vulpibus. So apes or apis, apis, apium, or apũ: vepres is of the common gender. sepes, trabes, plebes, are also thus contracted, seps, trabs, plebs: and adipes, of the common gender, being contracted, is adeps. These want the plurall number, indoles, strues, lues, fames, tabes, pubes: soboles and labes doe want the genitive & the dative case plurall. Verres is of the masculine gender: torques, and vates, vatium or vatum are of the common gender, panaces of the neuter : Senex an adjective, at the least in the

singu-

singular nũber. Certain Greeke nounes of this
end, are derived hither from the first declinatiõ
of even sillables: as Æschines, Æschinis, Ari-
stides, Aristidis : ꝙ certaine are declined also in
the first declination of even sillables: as Oron-
tes, Orontis, ꝙ Orontæ: Timarchides, Timar-
chidis, and Timarchidæ: And the genitive case
is sometimes taken from the second declination of even sillables : as Immitis Achilli : also
Duri miles Vlissi: of Achilles, and Vlysses.

Is, is: as *Corbis, corbis, corbi, corbem, corbis, corbe:
corbes, corbium, corbibus, corbes, corbibus.*

Araris which hath also Arar, stipis, scobis,
(whereof commeth stips, Scobs) strigilis, of the
ablative strigili, ratis, novalis, Buris, Præne-
stis. hic mugilis, ꝙ mugil, of the ablative mu-
gili: these following want the plurall number,
sitis, bilis, cannabis.

The *case.* This word vis hath in the singular
number onely vis, vis, vim, vi, but in the plurall
number it is fully declined: Vires, virium, viri-
bus, Vicem, vice, vices, vicibus, a word of foure
cases: ambage, ambages, ambagibus. gratis,
grate, grates. words of three cases,

Some nounes of this declination in the accusative case do end in *im,* as Ararim, aqualim,
securim, sitim, ravim, tussim, cucumim, bu-
rim, pelvim. So likewise many Greeke words.
But ofttymes they have *n,* for *m:* as Syrtis, Sir-
tin: Mysis, Mysin: Thais, Thain: Tigris: Tigrin:
Tyberis, Tyberin: Daphnis, Daphnin: Paris,
Parin.

Parin. Some have *em* oʒ *im*: as restis, febris, navis, turris, clavis, puppis.

When the accusative doth end in *em*, oʒ *im*, the ablative shall end in *e*, oʒ in *i*: as reste, resti: febre, febri: ȝ such like: to whõ are added these that follow, amnis, anguis, avis, ovis, neptis, classis, ignis, unguis, uectis, fustis, finis, civis. Which notwithstandyng foʒ the most part, do end in *e*: those woʒdes have onely *e* in the ablative case, whose accusative endeth onely in *im* oʒ *in*: as foʒ example: Neapolin, Neapoli: Thetin, Theti, Tigrin, Tigri: hunc cucumim, cucumi: pet Ararim hath Arare.

To this rule doe perteine those masculines, which seeme to be made of adjectives, as Annalis, annali: so affinis, Aprilis, Sextilis, sodalis, rivalis, familiaris, Quintilis: rudis, of the feminine gender hath onely rude.

But pʒoper names are agreeyng to the rule: as Laterensis, Laterense: Iuvenalis, Iuvenale: Martialis, Martiale. The nominative case plurall is Sardis, trallis, not Sardes, Tralles.

These woʒds are cõtracted in ȳ genitive plurall: strigilis: strigilũ: juvenis, iuvenũ: volucris, a bird, volucrum: canis, canum: panis, panum.

The gẽder. These nounes followyng are onely of the masculine gender, assis, ȝ the cõpoundes therof, octussis, semissis, tressis, decussis, centussis, vigessis: so acinacis, aqualis, axis, ensis, orbis, majalis, natalis, jugalis, retis, vermis, vectis, fascis, follis, fustis, and divers other en-

Lienis, nis, crini vnguis.

dyng

ding in *is*.mesis,torris,caulis,cassis,callis,cen-
chris,for a serpent,collis, piscis,postis : & these
three wordes,antes,manes, penates, want the
singular number : but these nounes following
are of the common gender:amnis,anguis,finis,
funis,ciuis,hostis,sentis,scrobis(wherof commeth scrobs) torquis , canalis, canis , clunis:
likewise also the first end of adjectives, tristis,
dulcis,whose neuters do end in *e*.

Nounes in *er* that are of this declination,are
of the masculine gender: as venter , ventris,
ventri,ventrem,venter,ventre:ventres , ven-
trum,ventribus, ventres,ventres, ventribus:
so vter, vtris, vtrum : imber , hath in the ablative case imbre, or imbri , yet the compoundes
of it have onely *i* , in the ablative case , as Sep-
tember,October, November, December: so
are Latine wordes in ter declined : as accipi-
ter,accipitris:frater,fratris: linter, lintris:lin-
trium , is of the common gender , the Greeke
word mater, matris, is of the feminine . Thus
are some adjectives declined,alacer, alacris: a-
cer,acris:equester,equestris:saluber,salubris,
volucer, volucris, celeber, celebris, and other
such like endes of adjectives , which all have
their ablative case , in *i*.

The rest which have onely *e* in the ablative
case , are alwayes contracted in the genitive
plurall,as fratre,fratrûm:matre,matrûm:pa-
tre,patrûn .

CAP.

Cap. 2.

The second declination of uneven sillables.

THe second declination of uneven sillables is that, whose Genitive case singular doth increase : and it is of Nounes of the masculine Gender.

The Greeke Genitive case ending in *os* short, doth here very often remaine : *Ovid. 2. Metamorph.* --- *silvas Erymanthidos ambit.*

And the Dative case doth sometimes make *i.* short : as *Catul.*

Morte ferox Theseus, qualem Minoidi luctum Obtulerat. -- For *Ovid* in *OEnon,* hath *Nympha suo Paridi.*

Of the Greeke Genitive and Accusatiue cases, there are formed some wordes of even sillables : as of Elephas, elephantis, commeth eliphantus, elephanti. of cassis, cassidis commeth cassida, cassidæ.

The Ablative of Adjectives of one end, endeth in *e* or *i*: as amans, amante, amanti: so Artifex, uber, supplex, vetus, fœlix, degener: after which sort these contractes following, doe end. Arpinas, fulginas, cuias, which have ended in *atis*, and *ate*: so the Comparatives, doctior, doctius: fortior, fortius: so verbals ending in *trix*: as ultrix, victrix: hospes, sospes, and pauper, have *e* alone : but proper names of Adiectives are

are regular: as Clemente, felice,

The Greek nominative case plurall maketh es short, and the accusative in *as*: Garamantes, garamantas,

The *neuters* that ende in *e*, in the *ablative case* doe forme the *nominative plurall* in *a* : as Corpore, corpora: Poemate, poemata,

But if the *ablative* ende in *i*, the *nominative plurall* hath *ia*: as Concordi, concordia : fœlici, fœlicia . Yet wordes of the *comparative degree* take away *i* : as Doctiora, plura, & complura (though there be also compluria) so doth vetera.

The *genitive case plurall* of an *ablative* that is *regular*, is evermore *contracted*: as honore, honorûm : milite, militûm . Cæsare, cæsarûm: passere, passerûm: doctiorûm, and of all other *camparatives*.

The increasing of the *cases* is distinguished by *vowels*: of which *vowels*, *a* and *o* are long: *e, i, u, y,* are short.

Those which doe increase by *a*, are neuters. *as, aris*, and in the plurall, *arium, aribus*, in some auncient wryters: yet Præs, prædis, is the *masculine*, and Fæx, fæcis, the *feminine gender* . So likewise is Laus, laudis: fraus, fraudis : & fauces, faucium, without the singular number.

As, asis: as Vas, vasis, of the singular number onely. But As, assis, assium,

As, aris : as Mas, maris, marium, is of the masculine gender.   Ar.

Ar, aris : as Pulvinar, pulvinaris : so these nounes Laquear, lucar, calcar, which are contracted & therfore end in *i* in the ablative:Nar, naris, is sometimes also a neuter, but jubar, jubaris, nectar, nectaris, bacchar, baccharis, an herbe (which also hath baccharis) have no plurall nuber.Hamilcar,hamilcaris: Cæsar,cæsaris:lar,laris,larium:also Lar,lartis,the name of a man : so the Adjective Par, paris, and the compoundes therof,Impar,separ,dispar,compar:far,faris,without the genitive and the dative plurals.

Al, alis : as Minutial, minutialis : cervical, cervicalis: which wordes seeme to be contracted of the neuters ende in *le*, as these that follow.Animal,vectigal,tribunal, puteal, which therefore have *i* in the Ablative case . Ispal, though it be the name of a Citie,yet it is of the neuter gender.

Nounes of the masculine gender doe make *a* short: Asdrubal,asdrubalis. Hannibal,hannibalis : sal,salis, beeing fullye declined in both numbers, is of the masculine,and wanting the plurall,is of the neuter gender.

An, anis: as Titã,titanis,pæã,pæanis. but caro,carnis, carnium,is of the feminine gender.

A, atis, is a Greek end: as Thema,thematis, poëma,poëmatis : so Zeugma (though it be the name of a Citie) which in the ablative and Dative case plurall are declined, as wordes
of

of the declination of even sillables, after the
AEO-like maner: as Emblematis, poëmatis,
hepar, hepatis, wanteth the plurall number.

As, atis, is of the feminine gender: as civitas,
civitatis, civitatium, and civitatum: for wordes
of many sillables ending in *as*, are oftentimes
contracted. So likewise are declined these that
have the plurall number, caritas and facultas.
So are bonitas, probitas, and such like substantiues, which are seldome used in the plurall
nūber. yet anas hath anatis with *a* short. These
two Adiectiues, nostras & vestras, are regular.

Ars, artis: as nounes of the feminine gender:
Ars, artis, artium: pars, partis, partium: whose
compoundes do chaunge *a* into *e*.

Ans, antis: as amans, amantis, an Adiectiue:
sextans, dodrans, quadrans, are of the masculine gender. So Adamas, elephas, acragas, cal-
chas, garamas, and such like Greeke wordes.

Ax, actis: as Astyanax, astianactis: Hylax, hy-
lactis.

As, adis, with *a* short, of the masculine gender,
as Vas, vadis : so certaine Greeke wordes not
only of the masculine gēder, as Arcas, arcadis,
arcadū, but also of the feminine, as decas, deca
dis: monas, monadis: so Doras, Dipsas, Pallas:
Nounes that betoken parentage, as Ætias, æti-
adis, Phaëtontias , Phaëtontiadis & such like,
Glans, glandis , glandium, is of the feminine
gender.

Femi=

Feminines which end in *ax*, have *acis*, with *a*, long: as Fornax, fornacis, fornacium: but abax abacis: smilax, smilacis: panax, panacis, have *a* short. Pax, pacis, wanteth the Genitive and dative cases plurall: so the Adiectives, audax, capax, fallax, and such like.

The rest of the wordes of many sillables that end in *ax*, are of the masculine gender. as Thrax thracis. But those which do follow do make *a*, short: Atax, atrax, anthrax, Syphax, syphacis, with *a* long, or syphacis with *a* short, styrax, dropax, colax, candax, pharnax, limax, limacis, and calx, calcis, for a part of the foote, are of the common gender, but calx, for bricke, is of the feminine, and so are lanx, lancis, lancium: phalanx, phalangis: arx, arcis, arcium: falx, falcis, falcium: but Briax, briacis is of the masculine gender.

Abs, *abis*: as Arabs, arabis. trabs, trabis, trabium, of the feminine gender.

Aps, *apis*: as Laelaps, laelapis : daps, dapis, dapium, both of the feminine gender.

Nounes which increase by *e*. Certain Greek nounes which are neuters: as Argos, epos, melos, hippomanes, cacoethes, should be declined after the Greeke maner, in *eos* pure: but in Latine they are so declined.

Some of the feminine gender in *es*, are so declined that *i* alone maketh the sillable of the increase: as Res, rei, rei, rem, res, re : Res, rerum, rebus,

rebus,res,rebus.

The genitive case singular onelye in nounes of the feminine gender thus declined, is lyke the dative, and hath *ei*, for *eis*, with *e* long, if *i* come betweene two vowels, as Species, specici:facies,faciei:otherwise it is short:as Plebs plebei:fides,fidei:spes,spei:whereof commeth that adjective of one case,Exspes.Dies,diei,is of the common gender in the singular number, and in the plurall, it is onely of the masculine gender:but Meridies is onely of the masculine gender. And manye of these nounes hauing *es* turned into *a*, are declined after the firste declination of even sillables: as I uxuries,luxuriei, and luxuria,luxuriæ. The plurall number except it be of Res and dies, is here seldom used.

Some nounes which ende in *es*, haue *eris* : as Ceres,cereris.

Is,iris:as Cinis,cineris:pulvis,pulveris.

us,eris of the neuter gender : holus,onus, o-pus, acus, aceris, hulcus, sidus,scelus,rudus, latus,munus,vellus,viscus,vulnus,fœdus,fu-nus,pondus:venus,veneris:vetus,veteris,an adiectiue.

Er,eris : Anser,anseris : later,lateris:carcer, carceris:passer,passeris : vomer or vomis,vo-meris: These adjectives,Huber, degener and pauper,make huberum,degenerum, paupe-rū,in the genitive plurall,Luceres,& proceres, without the singular number: yet *Iuvenal* said, Agnosco

Agnosco procerem - - -

Adde herevnto these that follow (although they be the names of trees) hoc siler, sileris: hic or hæc, or hoc suber, suberis : but mulier, mulieris is of the feminine gender.

These Greeke nounes, Aer, aeris, æther, ætheris, which want the plurall number, and crater, crateris, follow the Greeke declination and *prosodie*: so Character, characteris, and all others that end in *er* beeing long, which happeneth as often as the genitive doth end in *eris*.

The gender. Those wordes which doe signifie the fruites of the earth, and end in *er*, are without the plurall number: as Siser, siseris, (yet *Plinie*, in his 20. booke, and 5. chapter, sayd, *Hicesius ideo stomacho utile videtur, quoniam nemo tres siseres edendo continuaret*) Laser, cicer, papaver, both for the plant and the fruite, piper, hic vel hæc tuber, for the fruite of a tree : hæc laver, in *Plinie* : but hic cucumer, or cucumis: so acer, aceris, althogh it be the name of a tree, and that which heretofore was called itiner, and now iter, itineris: vber, vberis, the substantive, be of the neuter gender : so spinter, of juger, beeing out of use in the nominative case, commeth jugeris, jugere, in the singular number, and in the plurall it hath all cases : ver, veris, without the plural number: cadaver is perfect in both numbers : so of verber, which is rare in use, the other cases are usuall.

El,

El,beeing long, maketh *elis* : as Raphaël,raphaëlis:ſo Daniël,Michaël, and theſe neuters, mel,mellis,wanting the Genitiue and Datiue caſe plural,and ſel, without the plural number.

Ems,emis:as Hyems, hyemis,of the feminine gender.

o Long maketh *enis*: as Anio,anienis:Nerio, nerienis,the wife of *Mars* , whereof commeth Neriene,nerienes,and neria,neriæ.

En,enis: as Attagen, attagenis:ſplen, lien,lichen,and ſiren,ſirenis, of the feminine gender, whereof commeth Sirena,ſirenæ.

Es,etis,with *e*, ſhort : as hæc ſeges, teges,interpres, and indiges, are of the common Gender:hebes,teres,perpes,præpes,are adiectiues in the ſingular number.   But aries and paries are maſculines:Abies,a feminine: impetis,impete,impetibus, a worde of three caſes, and of the maſculine gender.Some do end in *etis*,with *e* long:as theſe nounes of the feminine gender, quies,quietis, and requies, requietis, and requiei :ſo theſe Adiectiues in the ſingular number,inquies,locuples:ſo Greeke nounes of the maſculine gender in *es*,as Lebes,lebetis,magnes,tayes,and proper names,as Mendes,mendetis,and mendis,ſo Thales,thaletis,and thalis:Chremes , chremis, & chremetis:and ſuch like.ſo Cæres, cæretis, and cæritis:of the common gender.

Ens,entis : as Dens, dentis of the maſculine gender:

gender:Lens,lentis, and mens,mentis, of the feminine,bibens,bibentis:serpens,serpentis: rudens, rudentis:cliens,clientis : parens,parentis, parentum oʒ parentium , of the common gender:so adiectiues,amens,amentis:demens,docens,legens,audiens.

Ois,oëntis,as Simois,simoëntis : Pyrois,pyroëntis.

Ers,ertis:as Expers, expertis:so iners.

Es,edis, of this soʒt there are few:as Pes,pedis.ǫ feminines:as compes,compedis,ǫ merces, mercedis, hæres, hæredis of the common gender:so befoʒe it was sayd, hic præs,prædis.

Ens,endis : as Libripens, libripendis, hic & hæc nefrens,hæc lens.

*Ex,ecis:*as resex,resecis (but halec, halecis, is of the feminine gender, and perfect in both numbers, oʒ els of the neuter gender without the plurall number) Myrmex,myrmecis: vervex,vervecis:but these nounes are of the feminine gender:Nex,necis; precis,precum,and other cases which want the nominatiue singular:fæx,fæcis:merx,mercis,are perfect in both numbers.

Ex,egis: as Aquilex,aquilegis:lelex,lelegis: grex,gregis:rex,regis : lex,legis, is of the feminine gender,whereof commeth exlex, exlegis an adiectiue . *Eps,epis:*as Seps,sepis a serpent.

⸿Woʒds increasing by *i:*as Glis gliris, glirũ.

D   Il,

Il,ilis: as sil,silis, a neuter. This word supellectilis hath heretofore beene used, whereof is
contracted supellex, supellectilis, and in the
ablatiue case supellectile, or supellectili, is a
feminine which lacketh the plurall number:
pugil,pugils,pugilum,of the common gender:
vigil,vigilis,vigilum ∶ so pervigil , are Adiectiues in the singular number.

O,inis: as Apollo,apollinis: turbo,turbinis:
so of those which doe ende in *do* and *go,* which
are of the feminine gender∶as siligo that wanteth the plurall number, also Lanugo,lanugi-
nis,which is perfect: so libido: formido ∶ yet
ordo,and cardo, are of the masculine gender:
homo and nemo (that wanteth the plurall)&
margo are of the common gender.

En,inis, is of the neuter gender : as omen,o-
minis, and gluten which wanteth the plurall
number: so nomen,fulmen,flumen ∶ but these
wordes that come of cano,are of the masculine
gender,to wit,oscen, liticen,lyricen, fidicen,
tibicen , (whereof commeth also fidicina,tibi-
cina)tubicen, cornicen∶so pecten, & flamen,
for a Priest.

Also heretofore hoc sanguen, and hoc pol-
len,haue beene used, but afterwardes hic sanguis,sanguinis, without the plurall number,
and hic pollis,pollinis,remayned in use.

In,inis : Delphin , and delphis, delphinis,
whereof commeth delphinus, delphini ∶ and
　　　　　　　　　　　　　　　　Salamin,

Salamin, which was also called Salamis, Sala-
minis, whereof came Salamina, salaminæ.

Es,itis: as ames, amitis : stipes, limes, fomes,
termes, tudes, trames, cespes, gurges, palmes,
poples: hæc merges : hic ꝗ hæc ales, antistes,
(whereof commeth antistita) eques, veles, miles, cocles, comes, Pedes, and Adiectiues in
the singular number hospes, sospes, (whereof
commeth hospita, sospita)also diues.

Is,itis: as Samnis, samnitis, samnitium : and
beeing contracted Samnitum.Dis,ditis: Qui-
ris, quiritis, quiritium, and sometimes also
quiritum: and feminines, lis, litis, litium: cha-
ris, charitis : cælites, wanting the singular
number, is of the common gender.

Vt,itis: as caput, capitis, a neuter : so occi-
put, occipitis: sinciput, sincipitis : and thereof
commeth these Adiectiues anceps, ancipitis,
biceps, bicipitis, præceps, præcipitis, which
are contracted of ancipes, bicipes, præcipes.

Es,idis: as the datiues of sedeo, which are of
the common gender: obses, obsidis: reses, resi-
dis: deses, desidis: præses, præsidis.

Is,idis: as lapis, lapidis: ꝗ cuspes, cuspidis, of
the feminine gender: and these Greek nounes
of the feminine gender, ægis, aspis, aclis, ibis,
tyrannis, cassis, capis, cenchris, a hauke, pyra-
mis, pyxis : so Greeke names that signifie parentage, and are declined after the greek declination, as Æneis, æneidos, and such like : yet

2   Cre-

Crenis hath crenidis, with *i* long: Nesis nesi-
dis, Psophis, psophidis. *Id, idis*, David, davidis.

Ex, icis: wordes of many sillables do chaunge
e into *i*: as apex, apicis: ramex, ramicis : latex,
laticis : vortex and vertex have vorticis, and
verticis: caudax, caudicis: and codex, codicis:
podex, podicis: but carex, caricis, and vibex,
vibicis with *i* long, are of the feminine gender:
and obex, obicis: imbrex, imbricis: silex, sili-
cis: cortex, corticis: culex, culicis: pumex, pu-
micis, are of the common gender. Adiectives
in the singular number, artifex, opifex, make
their genitive plurall artificum, opificum:
illex, illicis: but supplex hath supplices and
supplicia.

Ix, icis: as ibix, ibicis: calix, calicis: varix, va-
ricis, and such like. Cilix a man of *Cilicia*. But
these are of the feminine gender, histrix, salix,
filix, fornix, coxendix, pix wanting the plurall
number: natrix for a serpent, is of the common
gender : but these masculines following doe
make *i* long in the genitive case, spadix, phæ-
nix, pistrix for a fishe, and nounes of the feminine gender, as radix, lodix, cervix, perdix:
victrix, maketh also victricia, in the plurall
number: so do these Adiectives, foelix, pernix.

Ex, igis: as remex, remigis.

Ebs & ibs, ibis: as cælebs, cælibis: of the common gender. Libs, libis: a winde.

Eps, ipis, feminines: Forceps, forcipis: stirps,
stir-

ſtirpis, when it is taken foʒ iſſue, but beeing
uſed foʒ a plant, it is of the common gender:
princeps, principis, principum, is of the cōmon gender. Theſe adiectives, municeps and
particeps, have in the genitive plural munici-
pum , participum.

*Ix,ꝭuis:*as nix, nivis, of the feminine gender.
Thoſe that increaſe by *o.* Certaine Greeke
nounes are ſo declined, that the vowel *o* goeth
next befoʒe *is,os,ois:*as heros, herois : Minos,
minois.

*Os,oſſis:*as Os, oſſis, oſſium:ſo exos, exoſſis.

*Os,oris:*as mos, moris:ſo flos:but ros, roris,
hath rorium, in the genitive plurall. Glos is
of the feminine gender:os oris, orium, of the
neuter.

*Or,oris:*as rumor, rumoris:ſo honor, labor,
vapor, clamor, which have alſo honos, labos,
vapos, clamos, and ſopor which wanteth the
plurall number:primores, wanteth the ſingular number. Caſtor, caſtoris:rhetor, rhetoris,
and ſuch like Greeke nounes which increaſe
by *o* ſhoʒt. Arbor, of the feminine gender,
which is alſo arbos, arboris:author, authoris
and memor, memoris, are Adiectives in the
ſingular nūber:æquor, æquoris, ador, adoris,
(wanting the plurall number) and marmor,
marmoris, having *o* ſhoʒt, are neuters. Alſo cō-
paratives ending in *or* oʒ *us*, do make their genitive in *oris*:as doctior & doctius, doctioris.

Vs,oris,neuters,littus,littoris: so nemus, fa-
cinus, fœnus, tergus,tempus,decus,corpus,
(and Adiectiues hereof deriued, bicorpor, tri-
corpor)pecus,pectus,penus, pignus : lepus,
leporis, is of the masculine gender , specus,a
word of one case of the neuter.

Vr,oris. Of this declination there be foure
neuters,ebur or ebor,eboris:robur or robor
roboris,(euen when it is taken for a tree)jecur
jecoris,jecinoris,jocinoris:femur,femoris.

Ol,olis,as Sol,solis,the onelye worde that endeth in *ol.*

*O,onis:*as harpago,harpagonis:so aquilo,a-
quilonis,udo, ligo,titio, turbo, for a swoord-
player,cento,cudo: unedo is of the feminine
gender:but aleo doth seeme to the Grammarians to be a word of one case,Sulmo,although it
be the name of a citie, is of the masculine gen-
der:bubo,bubonis, is of the common gender.

In the time of *Cicero* and *Cæsar*,these Greeke
contracted nounes were declined after the Latine rule by *o* long:as Io,ionis: Dido,didonis:
Calypso,calypsonis: in the time of *Quintilian,*
the Greeke declination was followed : as Dido,didûs:Dido,dido:but I rather follow that
golden age.

Nounes which are deriued of verbs and end
in *io,*are of the feminine gender : as ratio,reli-
gio,legio,natio:so ditio and contagio (which
wanteth the plurall number)talio.But pugio

is

is of the masculine gender.

On,onis: as Triton, tritonis: trigon, trigonis: Agamemnon, agamemnonis: canon, canonis: but sindon, sindonis, and icon, are of the feminine gender: Python, of the common.

Os,ovis: as bos, bovis (of the common gender) and in the plurall number, boves, boum : bobus, and bubus. hic jupiter, jovis.

Os,otis: as nepos, nepotis: but cos, cotis, cotium: and dos, dotis, dotium: are of the feminine gender: and sacerdos, sacerdotis: compos compotis: impos, impotis, are of the common gender. But many greeke nounes encreasing by *o* long, are of the masculine gender: as Eros, erotis: Rhinoceros, rhinocerotis.

Ors,ortis: as these feminines: mors mortis: sors sortis, sortium (as also these Adiectives compounded therof, consors, exors)cohors, cohortis, cohortium: fors, forte: a word of two cases.

Ons,ontis: as Aaró, Aarontis: Phaeton, phaetontis: and such Greeke wordes.

Ons,ontis: as mons, montis, montium: fons, fontium : pons, pontium : but frons , frontiú, is of the feminine gender: spontis, spóte: a word of two cases: sons, sótis an adiective . *Os,* *odis:* as custos, custodis, of the common gender.

Certaine Greeke nounes do turne *us* into *odis:* as tripus, tripodis: so OEdipus, œdipodis: whereof commeth OEdipodes, œdipodæ: and OEdipus, œdipi.

Or, ordis: as cor, cordis, cordium: of the neuter gender: and the compoundes therof: excors, focors, vecors, concors, difcors.

Ons, ondis: as hæc frons, frondis, frondium.

Ox, ocis, with *o* long: as volvox, volvocis: and these Adiectiues, atrox, velox, ferox. But cappadox, cappadocis, hath *o* short: so celox, celocis, of the feminine gender: præcox, an adiectiue hath præcocis, and præcoquis: but nox, noctis, noctium, is of the feminine gender.

Ox, ogis, as Allobrox, allobrog s.

Ops, opis, with *o* long: as Cercops, cercopis: Cyclops, cyclopis: conops, conopis, hydrops, hydropis: but these haue *o* short, Æthiops, æthiopis: Cecrops, cecropis: Dolops, dolopis: Ops, opis, a Goddesse: but without the nominatiue case opis, opi, opem, ope, for ayde and power, and in the plurall number, it is wholly declined, opes, opum, for riches, whereof commeth the Adiectiue, inops, inopis, inopum.

Nounes that encrease by u.

Vs, uis: of the common gender: as sus, suis: grus, gruis.

Some nounes ending in *us,* are also declined with *us* pure for *uis:* as census, sensus, censui, censum, census, censu, censibus. So sinus which heretofore was sinum. These are of the feminine gender, acus, idus, wanting the singular number, ficus, a tree and the fruite, manus, tribus, domus, without *y* ablatiue singular,

lar,porticus,penus, wantyng the plurall number : but specus , and colus are of the common
gender.

Iesus,Iesu,Iesum,Iesu, Iesu, are cases taken
from the Greeke declination.

Some neuters ending in *u* are in the singular number but of one case.and yet in the plural
number are declined with diverse cases; as to-
nitru, tonitrua, tonitruum, tonitribus : cor-
nu,cornua,cornuum,cornibus,so veru,genu:
but these have onely the ablative case:astu,no-
ctu, jussu,injussu , permissu , promptu, in the
dative and ablative case plurall these end in u-
bus,artus,specus, lacus, tribus, partus , por-
tus,which also hath portibus.

Vs,uris: of the neuter gender: as rus , ruris:
so thus , without the genitive and dative case
plurall,jus,crus,pus,wanting the plural num-
ber:plus, in the singular number , wanteth the
dative case,and is a substantive,but in the plurall number an adjective,hauing plures & plura,plurium:Complures complura, and compluria, complurium, and hi lemures , lemu-
rum,do want the singular number : Ligus , Li-
guris , one of Liguria , is of the common gender : mus, muris, murium , of the masculine,
tellus,of the feminine.

Vr, uris, of the neuter gender : as murmur,
murmuris : so sulfur , guttur : so Anxur , and
Tybur , although they be the names of Cities

5   Anxur

(Anxur is sometimes also of the masculine gēder)but vultur,furfur,turtur, are masculines.
augur,auguris,fur,furis,are of the cōmon gen-
der:cicur,cicuris,an adiectiue.

ul,ulis: as præsul,præsulis:of the cōmon gender : so exul.

us,utis:of the feminine gender: as virtus, vir-
tutis:But salus,seruitus, senectus,juventus,&
such like substantiues , do want the plurall nūber: ỹ adiectiue intercus,hath intercutis,puls,
pultis,pultium,is of the feminine gender.

us,untis:as these Greeke names of Cities:O-
pus,Opuntis;Hydrus,Hydruntis: Trapezus,
Trapezuntis: Cerasus , Cerasuntis: names of
townes:so Aruns,arūtis:so these Latin words,
iens,euntis:and the compoundes abiens , obi-
ens , rediens , periens : yet ambiens hath am-
bientis in the genitiue case.

us,udis,with *u* long , of the feminine gender:
as incus,incudis : so subscus,palus, paludis,
paludium and paludum:notwithstandyng pe-
cus pecudis, with *u* short. laus, laudis, fraus,
fraudis,be of the feminine gender.

ud,udis,Bogud,Bogudis:

ux,ucis,of the feminine gender:as nux,nucis,
crux, crucis : but lux,lucis:wanteth the genitiue case plurall, Pollux, Pollucis:dux, ducis:
is of the commō gender : redux, reducis:trux,
trucis : fauces,faucium, faucibus , be adiectiues without the singular number.

unx,

unx,uncis : as Septunx, septuncis, septunci-
um: so deunx, deuncis, deuncium : quincunx,
quincuncis, quincuncium.

ux, ugis, as frux, frugis: of the feminine gender conjux (or conjunx) conjugis, of the common gender.

Bs, bis: as urbs, urbis, urbium:

Ps, pis, as auceps, aucupis: of the common
gender.

Nounes that increase by *y*.

Y, yos: as these neuters, moly, molyos : Æ-
py, Æpyos.

Ys, yos: as Phorcys, Phorcyos.

Yn, ynis: as Porcyn, Porcynis: Gortyn, Gor-
tynis, of the feminine gender.

Yns, ynthis: as Tyrins, Tyrinthis: a riuer and
a Citie.

Ys, ydis: as chlamys, chlamydis; of the feminine gender.

Yx, ycis, as Eryx, erycis: sandyx, sandycis:
calyx, calycis: Bebryx, bebrycis, a word beto-
kening a mãs countrie with *y* doubtfull, bom-
byx, bombycis, and lynx, lyncis : are of the cõmon gender.

Yx, ychis : as onyx, onychis: Sardonyx, sar-
donychis, of the common gender.

Yx, ygis: oryx, orygis: styx, stygis, a word of
the feminine gender.

Ybs, ybis: as chalybs, chalybis : of the masculine gender.

ps, yphis: as gryps, gryphis.   CAP.

CAP. 12.

Of Nounes that are infinite.

The generall rule of wordes of uneven sillables hath hitherto bene handled. There are but few nounes which are in number infinite amõg the Latinistes, as these neuters, frit, git, pondo: & these adjectives, opus, nequam, damnas: præsto: which wordes whether they be used in all cases, it is to be considered. So these nounes of the singular number onely, instar, fas, nefas, necesse, necessum, nihil, nil, gelu: but nauci & mancipi for mancipii are genitive cases, which will not have an adjective joyned with them, no more will frugi, for frugis: though *Cicero* sayd, bonæ frugi homo, such are ejusmodi, illiusmodi, huiusmodi, in which a speach is made one word by an accent. The names of numbers, being adjectives plural are infinite: as quatuor, quinque, & such as end in *a*, triginta, quadraginta, quinquaginta, sexaginta, septuaginta, octoginta, nonaginta: so cétum, mille, tot, totidē, quot, quotquot, aliquot: so *a,b,c,*alpha, beta, & all other names of letters. So wordes také definitly, as clarũ, mane, scire tuum. Some barbarous wordes are sayd to be infinites, as Adam, Noë, Aixi, Illiturgi, which in Latine might better be declined: as Adamus, Noëus, Aëxum, Illiturgũ, as *Cæsar* did decline the Frēch names both of men and

and townes, in Latine, as Orgetorix Orgeto-
rigis;Melodunum,Meloduni:such are sinapi,
gummis, cepe, Gadir, which might be better
declined, sinapis, Gummis, cepa,Gades. So
Cim might be made Cimum , & such like.And
thus much cōcerning the *etimologie* of nounes:
it followeth that we speake of a verbe.

The end of the first booke.

THE SECOND
booke of Peter Ramus
his Grammer.

Cap. I.
Of a Verbe.

A Verbe is a word of nū-
ber with tense and per-
son . A tense is a diffe-
rence of a verbe accor-
dyng to the times pre-
sent ,past, and to come.
Euery present tense
is passing,but not past:
The

The pꝛeter tenſe and the future tenſe are partly not paſt,ꝗ partly fully paſt . Therſoꝛe of this verbe finite there are thꝛee tenſes not paſt,ꝗ as many fully paſt , and every one of them almoſt are double . *The tenſe not paſt* , as the firſt pꝛeſent tenſe,amo,amor,the ſecond, amem,amer: the thirꝺ , amarem , amarer : the firſt pꝛetertenſe,amabam, amabar: the ſecond alſo, amarem,amarer: Of the firſt pꝛeter tenſe not paſt, ꝺoth ariſe a noune participle,bā oꝛ bar, beyng changed into *ns* : as of amabam, ſedebam, loquebar,commeth amans,ſedens,loqués. The firſt future,amabo, amabor : the ſecond,ama, amare,amato,amator . yet amem , and amer, may alſo be of the future tenſe,as well as amarem , and amarer . The ſecond and the thirꝺ perſon ſingular of the ſecond future is all one: as amato,amator.

   The tenſes fully paſt: as the firſt pꝛeter tenſe, amavi:the ſecond,amaverim: the thirꝺ, amaviſſem : the fourth amaverim: the future amaverim , oꝛ amavero : and in the other perſons , as in the ſecond pꝛeterperfectenſe. Foꝛ this is alſo ambiguous,as amem and amarem.

   The ſyllables of tenſes increaſing by *a, e, o*, are maꝺe long : as amabam , amatote , legemus. yet *e* befoꝛe ram,rim,ꝗ ro,is made ſhoꝛt. *i* and *u* are ſhoꝛt: as amaverā,amaverim,amavero,amamini,legitis,ſumus , volumus, perculi,pepuli: yet the *Poetes* , in amaverimus, a

mave-

maveritis, and such like, doe at their pleasure make long the last sillable but one.

The first preterperfecttense is made of the second person of the presenttense, the last letter *s* being turned into *vi*: as amas,amavi; fles, flevi;petis,petivi;audis,audivi.

The cōtraction of the first preterperfectense & the derivatives thereof, is most usuall & doth extend to the greatest part of verbes: as cupij, audij,amasti, nosti,scisti; & in the plurall number,as amavere,docuere,petivere,audivere.

The chief *Anomalie* of the preter perfectense is double, the first when *v* is turned into *u*, the vowell going before being taken away, as domus,domui for domavi: so habes, habui; alis,alui;salis,salui.

The second *Anomalie* is, whereas *v* is taken away with the vowell going before: as juvas, juvi;moves,movi:defendis,defendi:comperis,comperi.

The first person of the preterperfectense being of two sillables, is made long: as in flavi, movi,sevi,scivi.

And thus much concerning the tenses of a finite verbe. *A verbe infinite* is either perpetuall, or participiall. *Perpetuall* which is varied by *re, ri*,or *se*: by *re*, or *ri*,in the present tense. as amare,amari: by *se*, in the pretertense not past, the preterperfectense, and in the preterpluperfectense,as amavisse, *Participiall*, which is declined
like

like a noune that hath cases, and is either a
Gerunde, o2 a Supine.

A *Gerunde*, which in the p2esent tense and p2e-
tertise is varied in *di*, and *do*, and in the future
tense, in *dum*. The first is formed by chaunging
bam, o2 *bar*, into *ndi*: as amabam, amandi: sedebam, sedendi: loquebar, loquendi: Of the first
gerunde ending in *di*: the two other, endyng in
do, and *dum*, do arise. Of a gerunde doth come a
noune gerundive ending in *dus, da, dum*. Cicero,
Quibus tuendus erat. A Deo nobis causa or-
dienda est.

A *Supine* is that which is varied in the p2esēt
tense and the p2etertense in *u*, and in the future
tense in *um*: as amatu, amatum.

The first *Supine* is formed of the first finite
p2eterperfectense, the two last letters beyng
chaunged into *tu*, as amavi, amatu, juvi, jutu:
flevi, fletu: movi, motu: petivi, petitu: audivi,
auditu: this *ui* is chaunged into *itu*: as domui,
domitu: habui, habitu: alui, alitu: salui, saltu,
fo2 salitu: from hence doth p2oceede a noune
participiall ending in *us*, as amatus.

The second *Supine* is made of the first, *m* being added thereunto, as of amatu, amatum: &
from hence doth p2oceede the noune participiall ending in *rus*, *m* being chaunged into *rus*: as
of amatum, amaturus: and thus much concerning the *tense* o2 *time*.

A *Person* is a speciall end of a verbe: and is
th2ee-

threefold in both numbers: the first person singular amo, the second amas, the third, amat: The first person of the plurall number, amamus, the second, amatis, the third, amant, from hence there is a double forme of a verb, the first, is when the theame doth end in *o*, and if it may be varied by *or*, it is called a *verbe active*: as amo, amor: if it cannot, it is called a neuter: as sedeo, studeo.

The second is, when the theame doth end in *or*, and then if it may be varied by *o*: it is called a *passive*: as amor, amo: otherwise it is called a deponent: as Loquor. *Passives*, and *Deponentes*, do want their perfect tenses: but the supines of deponentes are formed of fayned pretertenses as: insidiatu, veritu, fruitu, mentitu, as it were of insidiavi, verui, fruivi, mentivi: hereof doth spring a noune of the passive or deponent signification, this letter *s* being added: as amatus, loquutus. Also the passive signification doth often agree to the deponent: as testata publicis literis: Meditata omnia,

Also certaine verbes are onely coniugated in the third person of the singular number: and they are called *Impersonals*: as pænitet, amatur: which wordes do follow the law of their originall theame.

CAP,

CAP. 2.

Of the first coniugation in bo.

THe varying of a verbe, according to tenses and persons, is called a *coniugation* : and it is either in *bo*, or in *am*: In *bo*, whose first future tense not past doth end in *bo* , or *bor* : and it is formed of the second person singular of the first present tense, by turning *s* or *ris* into *bo*, or *bor*: as amas, amaris, amabo amabor: sles, sleris, sle bo, slebor, & in the second persons of this future *e* is short in *beris* and *bere* : as amaberis, or a-mabere . The *coniugation* in *bo*, is double. The first , whose second person singular , of the first present tense doth end in *as* , being an active, or in *aris* being a passive . An example of the first forme is this.

Amo I love , amas thou lovest , amat he lo-veth: amamus we love, amatis ye love, amant they love:

Amem I may love, ames, amet: amemus, a-metis, ament:

Amarem I might or could love, amares , a-maret: amaremus, amaretis, amarent:

Amabam I did love, amabas, amabat: ama-bamus, amabatis, amabant:

Amabo I shall or will love, amabis, amabit: amabimus, amabitis, amabunt.

Ama, vel amato , love thou , amato: amate, amanto

amanto.

Amavi I haue loued, amavisti, amavit: amavimus, amavistis, amaverunt, vel amavere.

Amaverim, I might oʒ should haue loued, a-
maveris, amaverit: amaverimus, amaveritis,
amaverint.

Amavissem, I might oʒ should haue loued, a-
mavisses, amavisset: amavissemus, amavissetis, amavissent.

Amaveram, I had loued : amaveras, amaverat: amaveramus, amaveratis, amaverant.

Amavero I may oʒ can loue hereafter, amaverim, as befoʒe.

Amare, amavisse.

Amandi, of louing, amando, amandum : a-
matu, amatum.

The *Anomalie of tenses not past* ♦ Ovat is onely
used with Grammarians, wherof notwithstanding cōmeth ovans. of juro commeth dejero, ꝗ
pejero: Dor, der, ꝗ for are not used: daris, de-
ris, and faris, and those that spʒing of them, are
in use. Dabam, and those that come thereof, do
make shoʒt the first letter of the increase.

The *Anomalie of perfect tenses* : Of those that
are fully ꝗ regularly coniugated, there are few
Anomalies: Poto, potavi, potatu, & potu: neco,
necavi, necatu & nectu: plico hath sometimes
plicui, ꝗ plicitu·but foʒ the most part it is regular, as his cōpoundes are alwayes with sub,
oʒ with a noune : as supplico, multiplico, tri-

plico,

plico,seco and frico,have secui sectu, & fricui,
frictu : (but secaturus,affricaturus, refricatu-
rus, are good Latin wordes) veto,& domo are
of the first *Anomalie*,and juvo of the second: yet
Persius sayth vetavit and *Salust* juvaturus. La-
vo wantyng the pretertense hath Lavatum,
Nexo is sayd to want both the pretertense and
the supines : do,dedi, datum.

Of neuters some do forme nounes, as of a de-
ponent:as of inveteravi, inveteratu, invetera-
tus : so of juro, commeth juratus, of cæno,cæ-
natus,of titubo,titubatus.

These verbes following are of the first *Anomalie*,sono,tono,cubo,crepo:but sonaturum,
& intonaturum,are good Latin wordes:*Cicero*
also hath increpavit,& discrepavit.Mico micui:
emico,emicui,wanteth the supine,(yet emica-
turus,is in use)dimico, dimicui, & more often
dimicavi,but alwayes dimicatu,whereof commeth dimicatio:Sto, steti,statu: whereof commeth status,stata,statum : & status,status, sta-
tui:although there be also staturus, Asto,astiti,
astitu,and astatu:Præsto,præstiti,præstitu, and
prestatu,wherof commeth præstaturus, beyng
a word used of *Cicero*. Labo wanteth the preter
tense,and the supine.

An example of the second forme.

Amor, I am loved,amaris, vel amare, amatur;amamur,amamini, amantur.

Amer

Amer, I may oʒ can be loved , ameris vel amere , ametur : amemur, amemini , amentur.

Amarer, I should oʒ would be loved, amareris vel amarere. amaretur: amaremur, amaremini, amarentur.

Amabar , I was loved, amabaris vel amabare, amabatur : amabamur, amabamini, amabantur.

Amabor, I shall oʒ will be loved, amaberis vel amabere , amabitur : amabimur, amabimini, amabuntur.

Amare, vel amator, be thou loved, ametur: amamini, amantor.

Amari, to be loved.

All depouentes in this coniugation are fully regular.

Cap. 3.

Of the second coniugation in bo.

The second coniugation in *bo* is , whose second person singular of the first present tense doth end in *es*, oʒ *eris*, with *e* long.

An example of the first forme.

Fleo, I weepe, fles, flet: flemus, fletis, flent.

Fleam, I may oʒ can wepe, fleas, fleat: fleamus, fleatis, fleant.

Flerem, I might oʒ should weepe, fleres. fleret:

ret:fleremus, fleretis,flerent.

Flebam,I wept oʒ did weepe,flebas, flebat:
flebamus,flebatis,tlebant.

Flebo, I ſhall oʒ will weepe , flebis , flebit:
flebimus,flebitis,flebunt.

Fle,vel fleto,weepe thou,fleto: flete,flento:

Flevi,I haue wept , fleviſti,flevit, flevimus,
fleviſtis, fleverunt vel flevere.

Fleverim , I might oʒ could haue wept , fleveris , fleverit: fleverimus , fleveritis , fleverint.

Fleviſſem,I might oʒ ſhould haue had wept,
fleviſſes,fleviſſet: fleviſſemus , fleviſſetis, fle-
viſſent.

Fleveram , I had wept , fleveras , fleverat:
fleveramus,fleveratis , fleverant.

Flevero,vel fleverim , I may oʒ ſhall weepe
hereafter,and ſo foʒth.

Flere, to weepe.

Fleviſſe,to haue oʒ had wept.

Flendi,of weeping,flendo,fiendum.

Fletu,to be wept, fletum.

There are fewe verbes in this coniugation
that are in tenſes,and perſons fully regular : as
vieo,deleo, neo, and the compoundes of pleo,
expleo,impleo,repleo,compleo.

And fewer neuters,as oleo, olui , it ſeemeth
alſo to haue had olevi, wherof commeth oletu,
⁊ hereof are compounded exoleo,exolevi,exo-
letu:ſo aboleo,obſoleo,peroleo,(but aboleo,
abolui

abolui hath abolitu)ſo ſuboleo,ſubolevi,ſub-
olitu:but adoleo adolevi,adultu:redoleo,re-
dolui,and redolevi,redolitu and redoletu.

The firſt *Anomalie* in other verbes aſwell
fully coͤiugated,as neuters,doth containe a very great part:as arceo,arcui, arcitu: ſo habeo,
ſorbeo,moneo,taceo,terreo:but torrui, maketh toſtu: tenui, tentu: (but the compoundes
thereof, attineo, attinui, attentu: ſo detineo,
contineo)doceo,docui,doctu:cenſeo,cenſui,
cenſu: miſceo , miſcui, miſtu:timeo, timui,
wanteth the Supine.

Neuters:ſoleo,ſolui, ſolitu: ſo lateo, liceo,
libeo,valeo,mereo, noceo, doleo,aleo, coa-
leo,pario,pigeo,pudeo,placeo:but careo,ca-
ritu,and caſſu: frendeo, frendui, hath frenſu:
tædeo, tædui, tæſu, being out of uſe , whereof
commeth pertædeo,pertædui,pertæſu: pateo,
patui , paſſu : And very many neuters . hauing
their preterperfectenſe ending in *ui* , want the
ſupines: as egeo, egui, horreo, oporteo,hu-
meo , ſileo , ſordeo , ſtudeo, ſtupeo,ſtrideo,
ſplendeo , rauceo, rigeo , rubeo, langueo,
jaceo, vireo, vigeo , fœteo, fraceo , frondeo,
flaveo, flacceo , floreo, marceo , macio, mu-
ceo , nitio , tepeo , torpeo , tumeo , deceo,
candeo,calleo , polleo,putreo:Liqueo, licui:
ferveo, of the old verbe ferbeo, ferbui,wherof
coͤmeth deferbui, conferbui,& ſuch like:pæni-
tet is an imperſonall,and yet notwithſtandyng

4   pæni-

pæniturum, is *Quintilians* wozd.

The rest are of the second *Anomalie*, and have their supines almost regular : we will follow the endes of the pzetertense.

Si, su: as suadeo, suasi, suasu: mulceo, tergeo, but indulgeo, indulsi, indultu: torqueo, torsi, tortu: jubeo jussi, jussu.

Neuters: hæreo, hæsi, hæsu: ardeo, arsi, arsu: maneo, mansi, mansu: so remaneo : but emineo, and immineo, have eminui, and imminui, wanting the supines: audeo , wanting the pzetertense, hath ausu: wherof come these persons, ausim, ausis, ausit , ausint: so gaudeo , gavisu: but contrariwise the wozdes followyng want the supines: algeo, alsi: vrgeo, vrsi: fulgeo, fulsi: turgeo, tursi.

Xi, ctu: as augeo, auctu: so lugeo, mulgeo, mulxi , and mulsi, mulctu and mulsu: but luceo, luxi: frigeo, refrigeo, refrixi.

Vi, tu, are made of verbes that end in *veo* : as voveo, vovi, votu: so foveo, moveo: but faveo, favi , fautu : caveo , cavi , cautu : cieo , civi, citu.

These neuters following want the supines: livio, livi, flaveo, flavi, conniveo, connivi and connixi: paveo, pavi.

Di, su: as video, vidi, visu: spondeo, spospôdi, sponsu : mordeo, momordi, morsu, tondeo, totondi, tonsu: but there is also , despondi, remordi, detondi.

Neuters:

Neuters·prandeo,prandi,pranſu (whereof as it were, from a Deponent commeth pranſus) ſo ſedeo, ſedi, ſeſſu, and theſe compoundes,inſidio, obſideo· pendeo,pependi, penſu·but dependeo,dependi,depenſu.

Theſe want both the Preter-tenſe and the ſupines:aveo,ſalveo,ſtrideo,renideo,glabreo elueo,mœreo.

An example of the ſecond forme.

Fleor, I am wept for, ſleris vel ſlere,ſletur: ſlemur,ſlemini,ſlentur.

Flear,I maye or can be wept for, ſlearis vel ſleare,ſleatur·ſleamur,ſleamini,ſleantur.

Flerer,ſlereris vel ſlerere,ſleretur·ſleremur ſleremini,ſlerentur.

Flebar,I was wept for,ſlebaris vel ſlebare, ſlebatur:ſlebamur,ſlebamini,ſlebantur.

Flebor,I ſhall or will be wept for, ſleberis, vel ſlebere,ſlebitur · ſlebimur, ſlebimini, ſlebuntur.

Flere vel fletor,be thou wept for,ſletor: ſlemini,ſlentor.

Fleri,to be wept for.

Deponents of the firſte *anomaly* are almoſte theſe : Liceor,licitu· vereor,veritu · mereor, meritu·miſereor,miſertu tueor,tuitu: polliceor,pollicitu·but fateor hath faſſu· reor,ratu:medior wanteth the ſupine.And thus much of of the coniugation in *bo*.

Cap. 4.

Of the first coniugation ending in am.

A Coniugation in *am* is that, whose first futuretense not past endeth in *am*, oz in *ar*: and it is formed of the first person singular of the first present tense, this vowell *o* oz this sillable, *or* beeing chaunged into *am*, oz *ar*: as peto, petam: audio, audiam: petor, petar: audior, audiar: in whose gerundes, *e* in the middle of the word going befoze *u* and *d*, is chaunged into *u*: as faciundum, legundum, experiundum, from whence come such like Gerundives ending in *undus*. The coniugation in *am* is dubble: the first, whose second person singular of the first present tense doth end in *is*, oz in *eris* shozt: as petis, peteris.

An example of the first forme.

Peto, I desire: petis, petit: petimus, petitis, petunt.

Petam, I may oz can desire, petas, petat: petamus, petatis, petant.

Peterem, I might oz shoulde desire, peteres, peteret: peteremus, peteretis, peterent.

Petebam, I did desire, petebas, petebat: petebamus, petebatis, petebant.

Petam,

Petam, I shall or will desire, petes, petet: pe-
temus, petetis, petent.

Pete vel petito, desire thou, petito: petite,
petanto.

Petivi, I haue desired, petivisti, petivit: petivimus, petivistis, petiverunt vel petivere.

Petiverim, I might or shoulde haue desired,
petiveris, petiverit: petiverimus, petiveritis,
petiverint.

Petivissem, I might or should have had desired, petivisses, petivisset: petivissemus, peti-
vissetis, petivissent.

Petiveram, I had desired, petiveras, petive-
rat: petiveramus, petiveratis petiverant.

Petivero, vel petiverim, I shall or will desire.

Petere. to desire.

Petivisse. to have or had desired.

Petendi, of desiring, petendo, petendum.

Petitu, to be desired, petitum.

The anomaly of tenses not past.

Inquio, or inquam, inquis, inquit, inquiunt
The future, inquies, inquiet: inque, inquito
These verbes following, fac, dic, duc, are contractes, for face, dice, duce. So adduc, & præit
are compounded verbes (notwithstanding Terence sayde abduce, and traduce) but the compoundes of facio are regular, effice, perfice.
                                        Me-

Memento, and mementote, are the onely per‐
sons of the time or tense not past.

The *anomaly of perfect tenses*. These that fol‐
low are regular: as Sapio, cupio: and verbs en‐
ding in *so*, as arcesso, facesso, capesso: but there
is also sapui, facessi, and capessi.

These verbs do follow the first *anomaly*: vomo,
vomui, vomitu: so gemo, molo, dispesco, com‐
pesco: but alo, hath alui, alitu, and altu: gigno,
genui, genitu: so of lacio, allicio, elicio, illicio,
commeth *ui*, in the pretertense, and *itu* in the
supines (but of allicio, commeth allexi, allectu,
as illicio, pellicio) so pono, posui, positu.

These verbes following doe ende their Su‐
pines, by chaunging *ui* into *tu*: as colo, colui,
cultu: occulo, occului, occultu: consulo, consu‐
lui, consultu: this verbe sero, for ordino, and
the compoundes thereof, exsero, insero desero
consero: have servi, sertu: so rapio, rapui, rap‐
tu but linquo, hath liqui, lictu: so texo, texui,
textu: pinso, pinsui, pistu: inquisi and inquit
are onely used.

Neuters, strepo, strepui, strepitu: fremo, fre‐
mui, fremitu.

Verbes ending in *sco*, do borrow their preter‐
tense and their supines of their primitives: as
pertimesco, pertimui, as scisco, scivi, scitu: so
adscisco, rescisco, conscisco. Glisco wanteth
the pretertense, and the supines. Many neuters
borrowed out of everie coniugation, are of this
sort:

foʒt · as inveterafco , inveteravi , inveteratu-
convalefco, convalui, convalitu : ingemifco,
ingemui, ingemitu · obdormifco, obdormi-
vi, obdormitu. And if the pʒimitives do want
the pʒetertenfe and the fupine, the derivatives
ſhall alſo want them · vefperaſcit wanteth the
pʒetertenfe and the fupine. The compoundes
of cubo doe imitate both his pʒetertenfe and
fupines: accumbo, incumbo, decumbo.

Vi, utu : of which foʒt are theſe verbes that
end in *uo* · as arguo, argui, argutu : ſo imbuo,
imbui : delibuo, ſtatuo, ſpuo · luo, lui, luitu,
with Grammarians : but the conpoundes are
ablutu, and dilutu : alſo neuters · as ſternuo,
batuo. Notwithſtanding ruo, hath rui, ruitu,
and rutu, (whereof commeth erutu, and diru-
tu) Nuo, nui, nutu · ſo pluo, hath plui, and plu-
vi, plutu : nigruo, nigrui, ſterto, ſtertui, metuo
metui, tremo, tremui, without the fupine. The
reſt are moʒe unequall · as excello, excellui, ex-
celfu: antecello, præcello: meto, meſſui, meſſu:
nexo , nexui , nexu : pecto, pexui and pexi,
pexu.

Many other verbes are of the ſecond *anomaly* : in which verbes we will follow the endes
of the pʒetertenfe as it were the cauſes of the
fupines.

Si, fu: as ſpargo, mergo, tergo, rado, rodo,
lædo, ludo, trudo, divido, vado, claudo, plau-
do: of cello, commeth percello , perculfi, and
                                           per-

perculi,perculsu : so procello:parco,peperci,
parcitu,and parsu. viso hath onely visi.

Mitto,misi,missu : but quatio maketh quas-
si,quassu. so concutio, decutio,percutio : but
premo,pressi,pressu : This neuter cedo, hath
cessi,cessu,whereof commeth cedo,cedite : for
to tell.

SSi,stu : as uro ussi, ustu : gero, gessi,ge-
stu.

Xi,ctu: aspicio,aspexi,aspectu: and the rest of
the compoundes of specio, inspicio, respicio,
despicio,perspicio : so struo,struxi,structu: so
traho,veho,duco,coquo, vivo, fligo, and the
compoundes thereof affligo, infligo,confligo,
profligo,so sugo,suxi,suctu: rego,rexi,rectu,
and the compounded wordes thereof:as arrigo,
dirigo,porrigo,corrigo,whereof neuters contracted as pergo,surgo,assurgo,doe also make
perrexi,perrectu : surrexi,surrectu:so clango,
plango,tingo:so of stingo, commeth extinguo
distinguo : of ungo,inungo, perungo . But
pungo,hath punxi, and pupugi, punctu : re-
pungo,repunxi, and repupigi,repunctu : but
expungo,hath expunxi,expunctu : and com-
pungo,compunxi,compunctu : these wordes
following do cast away *n* in the supine:stringo,
strinxi,strictu:so fingo,pango,pingo . Mejo,
as it were derived of mingo, minxi, mictu:
lingo,linxi:ningit hath onely ninxit.

Xi,xu: as figo, fixi, fixu, so frigo, flecto, ne-
cto

&to,ple&to,fluo.But ango,anxi:conquinisco
hath onely conquexi.

*Psi,ptu.*as Sumo,sumpsi,sumptu: so scalpo,
sculpo,scribo,carpo,clepo,temno,demo,co-
mo,promo:in which it pleaseth some to write
p to make a good sound,saith *Priscian.*

Neuters:serpo,serpsi,serptu:so repo,nubo,
whereof commeth this worde nupta the bride.

*Ri,su:*as curro: cucurri, cursu: but accurro,
accurri, accursu : so recurro,decurro,præcur-
ro, (which notwithstanding with *Plautus*, is
præcucurri)verro, verri, versu:pario,peperi,
paritu ,& partu:furo,wanteth the pretertense
and the supine.

*Li,su:*sallo,salli,salsu:vello,velli,or vulsi,vul-
su:fallo,fefelli,falsu : tollo,whereof commeth
sustollo, sustuli,sublatu : pello,pepuli,pulsu:
of cello, commeth percello, perculi, and per-
culsu : so procello, proculi, proculsu: psallo,
hath onely psalli.

Mi,ptu : as emo,emi, emptu : adimo,ad-
emi, ademptu : redimo, redemi, redemptu:
but demo hath dempsi, demptu : promo,
prompsi,promptu.

*Ni,tu:*as cano,cecini,cantu: but accino,ac-
cinui, accentu:so occino, concino, præcino:
memini, in the Preterpluperfectense , and in
those tenses , which are derived of the perfect
(being called allied tenses)is coniugated.

Vi,tu : as sero to sowe, sevi,satu:insero, in-
sevi,

ſevi,inſitu ſo obſero:ſino,ſivi,ſitu : ſolvo,ſol-
vi,ſolutu:ſterno (as:were of ſtras) ſtravi,ſtra-
tu:ſperno,ſprevi,ſpretu:lavo,lavi, lautu & lo-
tu:voluo,volvi,volutu:lino,lini, livi, and levi,
litu:noſco,novi,notu:ignoſco, ignovi, igno-
tu:but agnoſco,hath agnovi, agnitu : ſo cog-
noſco,cognovi,cognitu:tero,trivi,tritu: cer-
no,and creſco,crevi,cretu : paſco,pavi,paſtu:
calvo hath onely calvi.

Ti,tu: as ſiſto,ſiſtis,an active,ſteti,ſtatu: but
the neuters, which are compounded thereof,as
obſiſto,obſtiti,reſiſto,reſtiti, conſiſto,conſiſti-
ti,do want the ſupine:verto,verti,verſu.

Di,ſu: as the verbes compounded of cendo,
accendo, accendi, accenſu : ſo incendo, and
ſuccendo : ſo ſcando, and the compoundes of
fendo, offendo, defendo : ſo mando, cudo,
prehendo:but ſido,ſidi,ſtrido,ſtridi, do want
the ſupines : ſido wanteth the pretertenſe,and
hath ſiſu,whereof commeth diffiſus, confiſus,
(*Livie* alſo ſayd,conſiderunt) fundo,ſudi,fu-
ſu: here are ſeuen verbes that doe dubble, as
tendo, tetendi, tenſu,and moʒe often tentu,
as in the compoundes extendo, intendo, o-
ſtendo, obtendo, diſtendo, portendo , con-
tendo:tundo,tutudi,tuſu: but the compounds
have obtundo, obtudi, obtuſu : ſo retundo,
contundo. Alſo verbes compounded of *do* : as
abdo, abdidi, abditu: ſo edo, reddo, vendo,
trado, condo (whereof commeth abſcondo,
                                    abſcon-

abſcódi)and moze ſeldome abſcondidi, recon-
do,recondidi)dido,dididi,diditu·perdo,per-
didi,perditu:ſo prodo,cædo, cæcídi,cæſu·oc-
cido,occídi,occiſu:ſo incído: pendo, pepen-
di,penſu·but perpendo, perpendi, perpenſu.
Neuters,as cado,cecidi,caſu: occido,occidi,
occaſu,recido,recidi,recaſu:accido,hath onely accidi,Pedo,pepédi, peditum. ſo oppedo.
The wozdes following doe dubble ſ: ſcindo,
ſcidi,ſciſſu : fodio,fodi,foſſu: findo, fidi,fiſſu:
pando,pandi,paſſu.

*Ci,ctu:*as ico,ici,ictu:jacio, jeci, jactu:injicio
injeci, injectu:ſo conjicio:vinco vici,victu:fa-
cio,feci,factu (faxo,oz faxim,faxis,faxit·faxi-
mus,faxiſtis,faxint,is uſed in the future) infi-
cio,infeci, infectu : ſo reficio,deficio: poſco,
popoſci,poſcitu· ſo expoſcitum caput (ſayth
Seneca)diſco,didici: diſcitu,ſayth *Priſcian* : ſo
repoſco,repopoſci:depoſco,depopoſci:ediſ-
co : dediſco, dedidici : foz the compounded
wozdes do here dubble.

Gi,ctu: as ago egi,actu· (whereof commeth
thoſe perſons,apage,apagite) redigo,redegi,
redactu· (but ſatago and dego, have only ſa-
tegi,degi)lego,legi,lectu:ſo relego, perlego,
(but intelligo,negligo,diligo, do make *xi* and
ctu) frango,fregi,fractu : effringo,effregi,ef-
fractu·ſo infringo,refringo,defringo: tango,
tetigi,tactu:attingo,attigi,attactu:contingo,
contigi,contactu·pago,pegi,and pepigi· im-
F   pingo,

pingo,impegi,impactu ſo compingo : fugio,
fugi,fugitu: ambigo,and vergo ,doe want the
pretertenſe,and the ſupines.

Bi,tu : as glubo,glubi,glubitu : bibo,bibi,
bibitu:but ſcabo.ſcabi.and lambo,lambi : do
want the ſupines.

Pi,tu : as rumpo, rupi, ruptu : capio,cepi,
captu:of the old verb cæpio,is made cæpi,cæp-
tu:whereof he is called cæptus,the which hath
taken.

An example of the ſecond forme.

Petor,I am deſired, peteris vel petere , pe-
titur:petimur,petimini,petuntur.

Petar,I maye or can be deſired, petaris vel
petare, petatur : petamur,petamini, petan-
tur.

Peterer,I would ſhould or ought to be deſired,petereris vel peterere,peteretur: peteremur,peteremini,peterentur.

Petebar,I was deſired, petebaris vel petebare,petebatur: petebamur,petebamini,pe-
tebantur.

Petar,I ſhall or will be deſired , peteris vel
petere,petetur:petemur,petemini,petentur.

Petere vel petitor, be thou deſired, petitor:
petimini,petuntur.

Peti,for peteri, which in all other verbes of
this coniugation,is made regular: as agi,legi,
duci

duci, and such like verbes.

Deponents are here greatly irregular : some haue *tu* in the supine: as of piscor, adipiscor, adeptu: so indipiscor: expergiscor, experrectus proficiscor, profectu : reminiscor commentu: obliuiscor, oblitu: ulciscor, ultu: sequor, sequutu: so loquor, loquutu : ringor, rictu: nascor, natu : nanciscor, nactu : fungor, functu: fruor, fruitu, and fructu : tuor, tutu, (whereof commeth obtutus) queror, questu : paciscor, pactu: proficiscor, profectu. The rest are in *su*: as utor, usu : reuertor, reuersu : labor, lapsu: nitor, nisu, and also nixu: fatiscor, fessu (wherof commeth fassus, defessus) gradior, gressu: patior, passu: but these words following want the supine: reminiscor, liquor, vescor.

Cap. 5.

Of the anomaly of Edo, Sum, Volo, Fero.

EDo, I eate, es, est: edimus, editis, edunt. So edam, essem, edebam, edam.

Es vel edi, eate thou: edite vel este.

Edi, ederim, ederam, edissem, edero, or ederim: esse, edisse: edendi, edendo, edendum: esu, esum: or estu, estum : but with *Seruius* both comedo: and also the passiue forme is fully declined. Yet estu, is used for editur.

SVM.

Sam, J am, es, est: ſumus, eſtis, ſunt.

Sim, J may oʒ can be, ſis ſit: ſimus, ſitis, ſint.

Eſſem, J might oʒ could be, eſſes, eſſet: eſſemus, eſſetis, eſſenr. Foʒ the ſame, forem, fores, foret: forent, ſo adforem, as it were adeſſem.

Eram, J was, eras, erat: eramus, eratis, erant: whereof is made the participle *ens*, which Flavius firſt uſed: but the compoundes abſens, præſens, potens: are moʒe uſuall.

Ero, J ſhall oʒ will be, eris, erit: erimus, eritis, erunt.

Es vel eſto, be thou, eſto: eſte, eſtote, ſunto: old wʒyters did uſe ſite foʒ eſte: as *Plautus,*

   Site mihi volentes propitia.

Fui, J have beene, fuiſti, fuit: fuimus, fuiſtis, fuerunt vel fuere. Of the old verb ſuo, whereof ſome examples are to be found, *Plautus.*

   Nec quiſquam tam audax fuat homo.

Fuerim, J might woulde coulde oʒ ſhoulde haue beene, fueris, fuerit: fuerimus, fueritis, fuerint.

Fuiſſem, J might woulde oʒ ſhoulde have had beene, fuiſſes, fuiſſet: fuiſſemus, fuiſſetis, fuiſſent.

Fueram, J had beene, fueras, fuerat: fueramus, fueratis, fuerant.

Fuero, vel fuerim, J ſhall oʒ will be hereafter.

             Eſſe,

Esse,to be.

Fuisse,to haue oz had beene

And of forem commeth fore : the onely futuretense of the infinitiue mood, which is perpetuall in the Latine tongue : so affore, deforе,profore: whereof commeth a future also.

VOLO.

Volo,I will,vis,vult: volumus,vultis,volunt. From hence come these contractes, sis,capsis,sultis:foz si vis, cape si vis, si vultis.

Velim, I maye oz can will, velis, velit: velimus,velitis, velint.

Vellem,I might oz shoulde will, velles,vellet:vellemus, velletis,vellent.

Volebam,I did will,volebas,volebat : volebamus,volebatis,volebant.

Volam,I shall will, voles, volet: volemus, voletis,volent.

Volui,I haue willed,voluisti,voluit: voluimus,voluistis,voluerunt, vel voluere.

Voluerim, I woulde oz shoulde haue willed, volueris, voluerit:voluerimus, volueritis,voluerint.

Voluissem,I might oz shoulde haue willed, voluisses,voluisset:voluissemus, voluissetis, voluissent.

Volueram,I had willed,volueras,voluerat: volueramus,volueratis,voluerant.

Volu-

Voluero vel voluerim, J ſhal will hereafter.
Velle, to will. Voluiſſe.

Compounded wordes do follow this rule: as Malo, Nolo.

Malo, J had rather, mavis, mavult : malumus, mavultis, malunt.

Malim, J maye oz can rather, malis, malit: malimus, malitis, malint.

Mallem, J might oz ſhoulde rather, malles, mallet: mallemus, malletis, mallent.

Malebam, J had rather, malebas, malebat: malebamus, malebatis, malebant.

Malam, J will rather, males, malet : malemus, maletis, malent.

Malui, J have rather, maluiſti, maluit : maluimus, maluiſtis, maluerunt vel maluere.

Maluerim, J might oz ſhoulde have rather, malueris, maluerit: maluerimus, malueritis, maluerint.

Maluiſſem, J might oz ſhoulde have had rather, maluiſſes, maluiſſet : maluiſſemus, maluiſſetis, maluiſſent.

Malueram, J had rather, malueras, maluerat: malueramus, malueratis, maluerant.

Maluero vel maluerim, J ſhall oz will rather, ꝛc. as befoze.

Malle, to have rather. Maluiſſe.

NOLO.

NOLO.

Nolo, I will not, nonvis, nonvult: nolumus
nonvultis, nolunt.

Nolim, I might oꝛ coulde nill, nolis, nolit:
nolimus, nolitis nolint.

Nollem, I might oꝛ should nill, nolles, nol-
let: nollemus, nolletis, nollent.

Nolebam, I did nill oꝛ would not, nolebas,
nolebat: nolebamus, nolebatis, nolebant.

Nolam, I shall nill oꝛ be unwilling, noles,
nolet: nolemus, noletis nolent.

Noli vel nolito, nill thou: nolite, nolitote.

Nolui, I have nilled, noluisti, noluit: nolui-
mus, noluistis, noluerunt vel noluere.

Noluerim, I have nilled, nolueris, noluerit:
noluerimus, nolueritis, noluerint.

Noluissem, I might oꝛ should have had nilled, noluisses, noluisset: noluissemus, noluis-
setis, noluissent.

Nolueram, I had nilled, nolueras, noluerat:
nolueramus, nolueratis, noluerant.

Noluero vel noluerim, I shal oꝛ wil nil. &c.

Nolle, to nill. Noluisse.

FERO.

Fero, I beare oꝛ suffer, fers, fert : ferimus,
fertis, ferunt.

Feram, I may oꝛ can beare, feras, ferat: fe-
ramus,

ramus, feratis, ferant.

Ferrem, I might or should beare, ferres, ferret: ferremus, ferretis, ferrent.

Ferebam, I did beare, ferebas, ferebat: ferebamus, ferebatis, ferebant.

Feram, I shall or will beare, feres, feret: feremus, feretis, ferent.

Fer vel ferto, beare thou, ferto: ferte, ferunto.

Tuli, I have borne, tulisti, tulit: tulimus, tulistis, tulerunt vel tulere.

Tulerim, I might or shoulde have borne, tuleris, tulerit: tulerimus, tuleritis, tulerint.

Tulissem, I would or should have had borne, tulisses, tulisset: tulissemus, tulissetis, tulissent.

Tuleram, I had borne, tuleras, tulerat: tuleramus, tuleratis, tulerant.

Tulero vel tulerim, I shall or will beare, &c.

Ferre, to beare: tulisse, to have or had borne.

Ferendi, of bearing, ferendo, ferendum.

Latu, to be be borne. Latum.

Feror, I am borne, ferris vel ferre, fertur: ferimur, ferimini, feruntur.

Ferar, I may or can be borne, feraris vel ferare, feratur: feramur, feramini, ferantur.

Ferrer, I might would should or ought to be borne, ferreris, vel ferrere, ferretur: ferremur, ferremini, ferrentur.

Ferebar, I was borne, ferebaris, vel ferebare,

re, ferebatur : ferabamur, ferebamini, ferebantur.

Ferar, I ſhall oʒ will be boʒne, fereris, vel ferere, feretur: feremur, feremini, ferentur.

Ferre, vel fertor, be thou boʒne, fertor : ſerimini, feruntor.

Ferri, to be boʒne.

Cap. 6.

Of the ſecond conjugation in am.

The ſecond coniugation in *am*, is whoſe ſecōd perſon ſingular of the firſt pʒeſent tenſe finite doth end in *is*, oʒ *iris*, with ꞓ long.

An example of the firſt forme.

Audio, I heare, audis, audit: audimus, auditis, audiunt.

Audiam, I may oʒ can heare, audias, audiat: audiamus, audiatis, audiant.

Audirem, I might would ſhould oʒ ought to heare, audires, audiret: audiremus, audiretis, audirent.

Audiebam, I did heare, audiebas, audiebat: audiebamus, audiebatis, audiebant.

Audiam, I ſhal oʒ will heare, audies, audiet: audiemus, audietis, audient.

Audi, vel audito, heare thou, audito: audite, audiunto.

Audivi, I have heard, audiviſti, audivit: audividivimus, audivistis, audiverunt, vel audivere.

Audiverim , I might oꝛ ſhoulo haue heaꝛo.
audiveris, audiverit : audiverimus, audiveritis, audiverint.

Audiviſſem , I might oꝛ ſhoulo haue had
heaꝛo , audiviſſes , audiviſſet : audiviſſemus,
audiviſſetis, audiviſſent.

Audiveram, I hao heaꝛo, audiveras, audiverat: audiveramus, audiveratis, audiverant.

Audivero, vel audiverim, I ſhall oꝛ will heare.
&c. as befoꝛe.

Audire, to heare.

Audiviſſe, to haue oꝛ had heaꝛo.

Audiendi, of hearing, audiendo, audiendū.

Auditu, to be heaꝛo.   Auditum.

The Anomalie of the preſent tenſe. 1 in the firſt
increaſing of this coniugation is long: as audimus, auditis.

In *fio* , ano in other perſons foꝛmeo thereof
the vowell *i* commyng befoꝛe another vowell,
is long: as fiam, fiebam: vnleſſe *r* follow: as fierem, fieri: from hence *Varro* ooth uſe infio, ano
the *Poetes* infit.

Onely theſe perſons of this verbe following
are in uſe , ajo, ais : ajunt: ajas, ajat: ajamus,
ajant,

The pꝛetertenſe not paſt, Ibam, ano quibam
after which ſoꝛte ſome haue pꝛonounceo other
woꝛoes: as nutribat foꝛ nutriebat, *Virgill* hath
alſo lenibat: *Catullus* hath.

Audi-

Audibant eadem hac leniter & leviter.

Ajebam , ajebas . &c. is here fully declined.
Fierem, fieres, is usuall, and not Firem.

The future tense not past, Ibo, and quibo . *
in aunciént writers, we read audibo , esuribo,
expedibo, as certaine others. *Propertius:*

   Lenibunt tacito vulnera nostra sono.

Horac . Mollibit aversos penates . of this word
ajo, commeth ai. *Plautus.* vel ai, vel nega,

Fito, and fitote, are used of *Cato* and *Plautus,*
but they are olde wordes .   Fieri , is taken
for fire.

The pretertense and the supine : Eo, ivi, itu,
queo, quivi, quitu; Haurio, haurivi, (but more
often hausi) haustu : amicio , amicivi , ami-
cui , amixi , amictu, aperio , aperui , apertu:
so operio , cooperio : but this verbe reperio,
hath reperi , repertu : and comperio , comperi, compertu.

Sarcio, sarsi, sartu: sancio, sancivi, sancitu , it
hath also , sanxi , sanctu : sentio , sensi, sensu,
sepelio , sepelivi , sepultu : sepio , sepsi, sep-
tu: vincio, vinxi , vinctu: farcio , farsi , far-
tu: fulcio, fulsi : fultu . Notwithstanding this
verbe ferio , wanteth the pretertense and the
supine . Odi , is onely used in the preterperfectense, and in the tenses of the same kinde : the
supine, at least wise of the compoundes is, osu,
whereof commeth exosus, perosus.

Neuters, Salio, salivi, salu, saltu : singultio,
                                                    singul-

ſingultivi, ſingultu: væneo, vænivi, vænu: venio, veni, ventu.

An example of the second forme.

AUdior, I am heard, audiris vel audire, auditur: audimur, audimini, audiuntur.

Audiar, I may or can be heard, audiaris vel audiare, audiatur: audiamur, audiamini, audiantur.

Audirer I might or ſhould be heard, audireris, vel audirere, audiretur: audiremur, audiremini, audirentur.

Audiebar I was heard, audiebaris, vel audiebare, audiebatur: audiebamur, audiebamini, audiebantur.

Audiar I ſhall or will be heard, audieris vel audiere, audietur: audiemur, audiemini, audientur.

Audire vel auditor, be thou heard, auditor: audimini, audiuntor.

Audiri, to be heard.

Deponens are regular: as ſortior, molior, blandior, potior. yet *Virgill* ſayd: Vi potitur.

Theſe verbes following are regular, to wit, aſſentior, aſſenſu: metior, menſu: ordior, orſu: but morior, moriris, moriri, and more often moreris, mori, moritu (whereof commeth moriturus) orior, ortu: Notwithſtandyng *Virgill* ſayd.

Exoritur clamorq; virum. *Horace.*

Nil

Nil oriturum alias, nil ortum tale fatentes.
So experior, expertu: opperior, oppertu: *Terent,* Horam ne oppertus sies: notwithstāding *Plautus* sayd, id sum opperitus.

CAP. 7.

Of an Adverbe.

A Word of number, is alreadp expounded: it followeth now, that we speake of a word without nūber, which over and beside his proper signification doth signifie no number: and that is an *adverbe,* or a *coniunction.*

An *Adverbe* is a word without nūber, which is ioyned to another word, as valde constans: differit acutè: benè manè. Therefore an adverbe is, as it were, the adiective of nounes, verbes, or of adverbes themselues.

There are fewe native aduerbes, mox, vix, cras, heri, ita, non: also interiections: as hei, heus, O, væ, pro: & *prepositions,* especially those which cannot be separated frō the word whereunto they be ioyned, as di, dis, re, se, am, con: *Di* is long, except in dirimo and disertus. *Dis* is put before three semivowels, *S, j,* and as many mutes *T, C, P,* as dissideo, disiicio, diffugio, (where *s* turned into *f*)distraho, discingo, disputo. *Di,* is put before the rest of the mutes.

And these are seperable prepositions: ad, apud, penes, and the rest, of which præ is made
short

ſhoꝛt in præit, and præuſtus. Per and præ being
compounded doe ſignifie great amplifiyng : as
perdoctus, prædiues ꞏ notwithſtanding, præ-
clariſſimum as *Cicero* his woꝛd.

Uery many adverbes doe ſpꝛing of nounes:
fixſt of thoſe which doe differ nothyng from
nounes : as theſe nominatiue caſes, utrum,
multum, minimum, potiſsimum : and as a-
blatiues, initio, veſpere, quo, qua, necef-
ſario, modo : and *o* being doubtfull, ſero, ſedulo, mutuo, cito, crebro.

Secondarilie adverbes are made of the ablatiue caſe, and that hauing diuers ends, diuerſly.
There are many made of the ablatiue caſe of a
noune ſubſtantiue ending in *im* : as of ſumma,
ſummatim, ſo of centuria, centuriatim, of
tribu, tributim: viro, viritim: of puncto, pun-
ctim : Some doe ende in itus ꞏ as of fundo,
funditus ꞏ ſo cœlo, cœlitus, of radice radici-
tus: ſtirpe, ſtirpitus. But the greateſt aboun-
dance commeth of the ablatiue caſe of an adiectiue endyng in *o* oꝛ in *i* ꞏ as of docto, doctiſ-
ſimo : docte, doctiſsime. Notwithſtandyng
bene male and rite, doe make *e* ſhoꝛt. Here
alſo ſometime the ablatiue caſe doth remayne:
as ſedulo, ſedule ꞏ ingrato, ingrate : ſometime
the ablatiue is chaunged into *itus* ꞏ and doth al-
moſt double, as diuine, diuinitus: publice, pu-
blicitus : humane, humanitus and humani-
ter, inhumane, inhumaniter of alio, commeth
aliter:

aliter : and aliâs, ignavè, ignaviter (but there is onely naviter)largè, lagiter ; luculentè, luculenter: firmè , firmiter.

If the ablative case doe ende in *i* , *ter beyng* added thereunto, it doth make an adverbe : as of acri, acriter : so sublimiter , and sublime: of forti,fortiter:facilè is onely used.Audacter, difficulter , are contracted . Omnino is made of omni . Those adverbes which doe spring of comparatives,do end in *us*,as of doctiori, doctius : of fortiori, fortius : yet of majori, commeth magis.

Those which doe end in *ns* do chaunge *s* into *:* as of amans , diligens , commeth amanter: diligenter notwithstandyng of repente , commeth derepentè and recens.

The adverbes of number, semel being excepted, are made of nounes. bis for duis (sayth *Tullie*)ter, quater, quinquies, sexies,septies, octies , novies , decies , undecies , duodecies , tredecies (the which is used with some as ter and decies)quatuordecies,quindecies, sexiesdecies, and in *Plinie* , sexdecies, deciessepties,and so forth vicies,tricies, quadragies, quinquagies , sexagies , septuagies , octogies, nonagies: so centies,ducenties, trecenties, quadringenties , quingénties,sexcenties, septingenties,octingenties,nongenties, millies :so quoties, aliquoties, toties : and those which end in am,bifariam, trifariam, quadrifariam.

fariam, multifariam, omnifariam, aliquotfariam: pridie, poftridie, perendie: nudiuftertius, nudiusquartus, and such like (as *Festus* doth say) are compounded wordes of die tertio, quarto, that is to say, now it is the third day, and now the fourth day: and they are alwayes spoken of the pretertense. 14. *Att.* Nudiuftertius dedi ad te Epiftolam. *Plautus, Mostel.* nam heri & nudiuftertius, quartus, quintus, fextus, usque poftquam hinc peregre ejus pater abiit. 5. *Phi.* Recordamini qui dies nudiuftertius decimus fuerit.

Cap.   8.

Of a Conjunction.

A *Coniunction* is a word without number, wherewith the partes of an oration beyng manifold, are ioyned together: & that is either *enunciative* or *ratiocinative*.

Speach. *Enuntiative*, whereby the partes of * an enunciation are ioyned: & it is partly *congregative*, and partly *segregative*.

Congregative, wherewith the partes being as it were true at the same tyme, are ioyned together: and it is either *copulative*, or *connexive*.

Copulative, wherewith the partes are coupled absolutely: as ac, etiam, item, nec, quoque que, and compounded wordes, atque, itemq;, neque.

Conne-

Connexive, whereby the * consequent is coupled upon condition of the ` antecedent : as si, sin, ni, nisi. That which followeth. That which wēt before

Segregative, whereby the partes of the enunciation, as being not true at the same tyme, are seperated : and it is either *discretive*, or *disiunctive*.

Discretive, wherewith the partes are onely seperated in reason. as autem, ast, at, interea, interim, ut, veró, verùm, nunc, tamen, etsi, tametsi, quanquam, quamvis : extraquam, præterquam.

Disiunctive, whereby the partes themselues, are so seperated, as if onely one of them could be true : as aut, an, sive, vel, ve, secus.

Ratiocinative, wherewith one part of reasoning is as it were prooued by the other, ⁊ that is called *causall*, or *rationall*,

Causall, wherewith the cause of the antecedent is rendered : as enim, enimvero, etenim, siquidem, quoniam, quia, nam, namque.

Rationall, wherewith the consequent is concluded of that which went before: as ergo, ita, itaque, ideo, igitur, quare, quamobrem, quapropter, quocirca.

The end of the second booke.

G   THE

THE THIRD
Booke of Peter Ramus
his Grammar.

CAP.   I.

Of the agreement of a Noune.

Timologie is expoun-
ded in her partes, now
Sintax is to be spoken
of. *Syntax* is the second
part of Grãmar, which
doth interpret the con-
struction of wordes,
whereunto a frequent
* *Anomalie*, being cal-

Vhich is
ot accor-
ng to rule.
)r want.

led *Ellipsis*, or * *defect*, is opposed . *Syntax* is either in *congruitie* and *agreement*, or els in *rection*
and *governement*. *Congruitie* is, when wordes do
agree in commõ properties, which first of all is
of wordes of number, whereof notwithstanding
there

there is a certaine exception:& this *Syntax* is of
a noune with a noune, and of *a verbe with a noune*.

The agreement of a noune with an other , is in
case, gender, and number , 2. Ep. Gravi teste privatus sum amoris summi erga te mei, patre
tuo clarissimo viro. Here are three substātives
teste, patre, viro, agreeing together, betwene
themselves in nūber gēder and case, & agreeing
likewise with their adiectives gravi tuo clarissimo, in number, gender, & case. As also amoris
summi, mei, agree betwene themselves, here
the first *Anomalie* is conunon by defect.

In the agreement of the *substantive* and the *ad-*
iective, the substantive sometymes, and some-
tunes the adiective is * concealed:but it may u- Not set
sually be understoode by some thyng that is ex- downe.
pressed. *Sal.* Exercitus hostium duo , unus ab
urbe, alter à Gallia obstant . Here is understood,this substantive exercitus, in these adiectives, unus, & alter . Clarissimo patre natus,
avis, majoribus . here is twise understoode the
adiective clarissimis, for the substantives, avis,
and majoribus.

The next *Anomalie* is of number. *Many sin-*
gular numbers are taken for one plurall. 2. *Divin.*
Procles & *Eurysthenes*, Lacedœmoniorum reges, gemini fratres fuerunt. But the *Anoma-*
lie of number in substantives is more common.
*Liv.Lib.*28.Celtiberi, novus miles : urbs A-
thenæ , which is also sometime in adiectives.

2   Pro

Pro Mil . Si tempus est ullū jure hominis ne-
candi, quæ multa sunt. In *Bru.* Quo uno vin-
cebamur a victa Græcia, id ereptum illis est.

Vhich
ath relatió
> some
ing be-
xe.

And there is no lesse libertie of the * reciprocatiue pronoune sui, ioyned with a gerund : but
notwithstanding it is very good Latin. 2 . *Divin.* Stoicos nostros irridendi sui facultatem
dedisse. *Cesȷ.7.* Liberam facultatem sui recipi-
endi Bellovacis dederunt . The speciall *Ano-*
malie of nounes, is in gender and case.

The *Anomalie* of gender, is either of one gender vnlike to another : or of many genders vnlike to one: of one, as in *Bruto, Scipio, Corculum.*
Cesȷ. I . *comm.* Garumna flumine . *Ter. And,*
vbi illic scelus est, qui me perdidit? Mors omnium rerum extremum, that is, res extrema.
The *Anomalie* of the gender hath great ele-
gancie when as the relatiue adiectiue Qui, betwene two substantiues of diuerse genders,
doth agree with the latter, whereas it ought to
agree with the former. I . *Leg.* Animal plenum
rationis, quem vocamus hominem. Notwithstanding here the * regular *Sintax* is approued.
In *Som.* Homines tuentur illum globum, qui
terra dicitur. 2 . *Nat.* Iovis stella, quæ Phaëton
dicitur . The same *Anomalie* is elegant in an
adiectiue deriued of a verbe. 2 . *Divin.* Non omnis error stultitia dicēda est. *Liv.* lib . 1 Gens
vniuersa Veneti appellati.

ccording
> rule.

There is also an *Anomalie* of many genders

to one. *The masculine and the feminine gender of thinges that have life, doe agree unto the masculine gender.* *Cæs,*Ptolomæum & Cleopatram reges. *Teren,Eun.*Pater & mater mortui.

But the diverse genders of those thinges which have no life, doe agree with the neuter gender: as I. Off. Pulchritudinem, constantiam, ordinem, in consiliis factisque conservanda putat.

The *Anomalie* of gender and also of number, in the same sentēce, is moze seldome. *Sal,*in jug. Maxima pars vulnerati aut occisi sunt : that is, maxima ex parte, vel plurimi vulnerati aut occisi sunt, as *Cicero* useth to speake.

The *Anomalie* of case is most rare: as *Cic, Att.* Macte vir virtute esto. *Liv.* 2. juberem macte virtute esse, si pro mea patria ista virtus staret. foz here macte is put foz mactus and mactum.

Certaine adiectives doe agree to certaine substantives: as these adiectives, which signifie numbers of dividyng, doe agree to those nounes substantives,which want the singular number. 6. *Att.* Binas abs te accepi literas. 4. *Verr.* Inter binos ludos, So Quisque with certaine degrees of comparison. *Cic, pro Com.* Quo quisque est ingeniosior, hoc docet iracundiùs & laboriosius. 1. *Tuscul.* Doctissimus quisque. 1. *Acad.*Recentissima quæq; . But *Cicero* sayth. 3. *Nat.* Omnia minima : & 2. *Orat.* Omnes tenuissimas particulas.

CAP. 2.

Of the agreement of a Verbe.

THe agreement of a verbe with a noune, is
in number and person, Ego, and nos, are of
the first person. tu, & vos, are of the second person. the nominative cases of other nounes are of
the third person. & the oblique cases of no person. frō hence the nominative case going before
a verbe is called the *supposite*, & the verbe the *ap-*
posite: as ego amo, nos amamus: tu amas, vos
amatis: Tullius amat, Tullij amant.

The *Anomalie of the supposite and the apposite.*
By the *apposite* of the first and second person,
is oftentymes understoode the *supposite* of the
first and second person. *Teren. And.* Ah vere-
or coram in os te laudare amplius. Here e-
go, is understoode. *Plautus.* Tibi aras, tibi
occas, tibi seris, tu is understoode. Also the
apposite is often understood of some thyng spokē
before. *Sal.* Exercitus hostium duo, unus ab
vrbe, alter a Gallia obstant, here is understood,
unus exercitus obstat, alter exercitus obstat.
The defect of the *apposite* beyng understoode of
nothyng that is expressed, is more rare. *Teren.*
Eun. Ego ne illam? quæ illum? quæ me?
quæ non? here is understoode, non vlciscar,
recepit, exclusit, admisit, also these kyndes
of

of speaches that are continually in use, as , sed hæc hactenus, quid multa?

The *Anomalie* of number is here lesse usuall. *Sal*, Cœpere se quisque magis ac magis extollere . and more rare is that and altogether poeticall. 1 .*Æneidos*,pars in frusta secant.

The *Anomalie* of number is more elegant in a verbe substantive , when as that doth agree with the latter of the *suppositos* , which ought to agree with the former: as *Terent.*in *And* . amantium iræ amoris redintegratio est. which is more usuall with Poetes : *Ovid* , omnia pontus erat . This *Anomalie* of number is also often used even with orators : *Orat* . Sin oratoris nihil vis esse , nisi compositè , ornatè , copiosè eloqui : quæro id ipsum , quî possit assequi sine ea scientia,quam ei non conceditis : for here , vis , and conceditis are unlike in number . Notwithstanding *Quintilian* doth thinke it to be a like solecisme or incongruitie , if one calling one man , should say venite , or lettyng many goe their wayes, should say , abi . But notwithstandyng the second person singular is for the most part so used . 1.*Orat* . Age verò ne semper forum, subsellia , rostra,curiam mediteris , for meditemur , or quispiam meditetur.

The *Anomalie* of persons is almost continually in use . *In nounes the first person , ioyned with the second or the third , agreeth with a*

verbe

verbe of the first, and also *the second*, *ioyned with
the third*, *doth agree with a verbe of the second
person*. *Terent. Adelp.* Hæc ſi neque ego neque
tu fecimus. *Cicero Terentiæ*, Ego & ſuauiſsi-
mus Cicero valemus, ſi tu & Tullia lux noſtra valetis. *Cicer.2. Philipp.* Defendi rempub-
licam adoleſcens, non deſeram ſenex. here
ego adoleſcés, & ego ſenex is the ſuppoſite of
the firſt perſon. 2. *Philip.* Hæc tu homo ſapiés,
non ſolú eloquens, auſus es vituperare. here
tu homo ſapiens, is of the ſecond perſon.

The gerunde in *dum*, and the latter ſupine
in *um*, are put in place of the *ſuppoſite*, in theſe
formes of conſtruction, *pugnandum eſt*, *pugna-
tum eſt.*

CAP. 3.

Of the agreement of wordes without
number, and firſt of an aduerbe.

The ſecond agreement is of wordes without number, as of the aduerbe or coniunction.

Sometime the aduerbe is uſed for the noune
relative: as, digna res eſt ubi nervos intendas tuos: that is to ſay, in qua. In like maner,
ille ipſe unde. Cauſa eſt cur, that is, quamobrem. Multa ſigna dederat, quamobrem reſponſurus non videretur.

Certaine aduerbes of compariſon and of nūber

ber habe a peculiar agreement.

This adverbe *quàm* may be ioyned to al the degrees of comparison. 7. *Ep. Quàm sint morosi qui amant, vel hinc intelligi potest:* 2. *Verr. Quàm audax ad conandum, tam obscurus in agendo. Cicer.* 2. *Orat. Perquam puerile.* But it doth eyther follow one comparatiue, oɽ els it is put betweene two: as *Tullius disertior quàm Atticus.* 13. *Ep. Non quicquam facio libentius quàm scribo.* 1. *Cat. Serius quàm crudelius factum. Quintil. lib.* 3. *Cap.* 14. *Salubrior studiis quàm dulcior.* With the superlatiue. in *Lelius* Habere quàm laxissimas habenas amicitiæ. 16. *Ep.* Quam celerrimé mittere. *Ter. Hecyr.* Quàm minima in spe situs erit, tam maxime pacem conficiet.

Vt is also ioyned vnto the superlatiue degree. 7. *Ep.* Vt gravissimè diligentissimequè potui.

Tam, somtime is of the same foɽce. in *Lal.* Vituperanda est rei tam maximè necessariæ incuria.

Longè and *multò* do agree to the comparatiue and superlatiue degree: as longè melior. 1. *Orat.* Principi longè omnium gravissimo. Multò commodiora. Pro *Manil.* Conspectus vester multò jucundissimus.

Adverbes signifiyng number, do agree with al nounes distributiues. 2. *Nat.* Vt bis bina, in *Somn.* Septenos octies solis anfractus.

CAp.

CAP. 4.

Of the agreeing of a coniunction.

THe agreeing of *coniunctions* consisteth almost in the order of going before, and comming after, or of them both.

Of *copulatives* these do goe before; atque, ac et, sed, sedetiam, verùm, verumetiam, nedum nec, neque, tum, quin, quinetiam. *Ter. Adel.* Tali genere atque animo. *Ter. And.* Parcé ac duriter, *Pro. Clu.* Explosum & ejectum, and so in other wordes.

This Coniunction Et from twenty to an hundreth, doth set in the former place the lesser number of nounes signifiyng number. 4. *Verr.* Ab hinc duos & viginti annos est mortuus. *de Senect.* jam tertius & trigesimus est annus. 4. *Att.* Septimo quinquagesimo die postquam oppugnare coepimus. *De Fat.* Morietur epicurus cùm duos & septuaginta annos vixerit. So in adverbes. *Plin. lib. 7. cap. 27.* Sit proprium Catonis quater & quadragies causam dixisse.

Onely quoque and que, are set in the latter place: *Pro Rab.* Me scilicet maximé, sed proxime illum quoque fefellissent. 3. *Tusc.* Balbutire desinant, apertéque audeant dicere.

Etiam, item, itemque, insuper, præterea, yel are common.

Of *connexives*, si, ni, nisi, are common: Sin is onely

onely put befoze. But mozeober all doe agree
with all finite tenses oz times. 2.*Frat*,Si perfi-
ciunt,optimè;sin minus,&c,10. *Att*.Si vir esse volet, præclara synodia : sin autem,&c. 1.
Cat,ni exeunt,ni pereunt.7. *Att*.Nisi ego in-
sanio. *Am*.Nisi apertum in pectus videas.
There is also an agreement betwixt this coniunction & the adverb fortè: si fortè, nisi fortè:
where foz y mott part al do erre oz are deceiued

Of *discretives* onely these following are put
befoze,ast,at,extraquam, imò,sed,quòd,præ-
terquam, quamvis, qnanquam. 1. *Att*. Tu
crebas à nobis literas expecta : ast plures etiam mittito. *Att*. Non cognoscebatur foris,
sed domi:non ab alienis,at à suis.2.*In*. Postu-
lat is quicum agitur,à Prætore exceptionem
extra quam in reum capitis prejudicium fi-
at.3. *Catil*. Nullum à vobis præmium postu-
lo, præterquam hujus diei memoriã sempi-
ternam,Quanquam and quamvis do agree to
all finite times oz tenses.*Pro Amer*.Quanquã
abest à culpa, suspicione tamen non caret.2.
Orat. Quanquam ita se rem habere arbi-
trentur,tamen,&c. *Pro Amer*. Quamvis ille
fœlix sit, tamen,&c.Notwithstanding Columella sayd *Hb*. 2. *cap*,7. Quamvis de mensura
minus convenit authoribus.

These following are put after,Tantum,au-
tem,interea,interim,verò. 11. *Ep*. Nil autem amabilius officio. *Pro Cluent*. Tum interea

terea nullum vestigium pecuniæ invenitis,
Pro. *Syl.* Quod sine eodem illo Catilina faci-
nus admisit, cum interim Sylla cum ijsdem
ipsis,&c.*Cic.*4.*Ep.*Ego verò servi vellem,

These are common, alioqui, alioquin, vt, licet, tamen, porro. Vt and licet, doe onely agree
vnto the second finite tenses, or times. 5. *Ver.*
Vt illud non cogitares: tamen, &c. *De respon.*
Quam volumus, licet ipsi nos amemus, tamen, &c.

A disiunctive is onely put before: aut bibat,
aut abeat, ve, is to be excepted. 6. *Attic.* Bis terve literas miserat.   An is sometime a disiunctive, but yet an interrogative: as 5 *Verr.* Erravit, an potius insanivit Apronius? vide utrum
vis argentum accipere, an causam meditari
tuam.

Of causals onelye Etenim, nam, namque, are
put before: enim onely is put after.

These are common, Enimvero, vt, uti, siquidem, ne.

Of rationals these are onelye put before . Sic
quas ob res, quamobrem, quapropter, quocirca.

These are common, Ergo, ita, itaque: igitur
is more seldome set before: *Sal.* igitur initio reges diversi, pars ingenium, alij corpus exercebant.

The *anomaly* in coniunctions is two-folde.
Polysyndeton, that is ioyning togeather of ma-
nie

nie coniunctions, and *Asyndeton*. *Polysyndeton*
is when a coniunction is superfluous. *Pro. Cal.*
Res tamen ipsa & copiose & graviter accusa-
ri potest. 5. *Tusc.* aut bibat, aut abeat. *Ter. And*
Sive ista uxor, sive amica sit. 16. *Att.* Etsi,
quamvis non fueris suasor & impulsor pro-
fectionis meæ, approbator certé fuisti. *Asyn-*
deton is when a coniunction is taken away. *Cic.*
Cat. Abijt, excessit, evasit, erupit. here the copulative is not expressed. 2. *Phil.* Tu cum prin-
cipem, Senatorem domi habeas, ad eum nihil refers, ad eos refers qui suam domum
nullam habent, tuam exhauriunt. here are
understood the discretives quidem, autem. 7.
Verr. Consilium capit primò stultum, verun-
tamen clemens. here etsi is not expressed. *Te-*
ren. Eun. Memini tametsi nullus moneas. here
is tamen understood. *Pro Mil.* Quatuor, ad
summum quinque sunt inventi. *Frat.* Velit, nolit, difficile est. here the disiunctive is not expressed. *Att.* nolim
ita existimes. here is understood the cau-
sal, vt.

The end of the third booke.

THE

THE FOVRTH
Booke of P. Ramus his
GRAMMAR.

CAP. I.

Of the rection of a Verb.

Or government.

THE *congruitie of a word* is briefly expoū-ded : there followeth *rection*, as when a worde doth governe an other word with a certaine end of varying : which first shall be in words of number, afterward in adverbes . And first of all in words of number, there shall be *rection* both of a noune substantive, and of a noune Adiective. The *rection* of a noune substantive is dubble : first, a substantive of the *adiunct* doth governe in the genitive case, a substantive of the *subiect*.

2. *At.* Cato dicit tanquam in Platonis politia,

non

non tanquam in Romuli fœce, fententiam.
here *Plato* is the subiect, to whom is adioined ƀ
doth happen politia. Sometime the word that
governeth is concealed. 2. *Phil.* Quod in tabu-
lis (quæ funt ad opis) patebat. Here ædem is
concealed. from hence doth arife a three-folde
conftruction: firft thefe genitive cafes, mei, tui,
fui, noftrum, noftri, veftrum, and veftri, are u-
fed as it were for the subiect. 5, *Att.* Vt ratio
mei, noftri. 1. *Ep.* Defenfor tui. 1. *Att.* de pre-
cator fui. 2. *Att.* fatietas noftri. *De pro.* Omniũ
noftrũ adolefcentiæ. 1 1. *Att.* Omniũ noftrum
bona. But ƀ poffeffives are moft often ufed for
the primitives. *Ter. Heau.* Quæ mea caufa fecit. *Am.* Quæ nunquam faceremus, *Pro. Am.*
Quæ fua caufa cupere ac debere intelligebat

Secondly, thefe poffeffives, meus, tuus, fuus,
nofter, and vefter, doe admit foure kinds of genitive cafes, as it were of the subiect, by the
fame conftruction. The firfte is of chiefe or
principall numbers. *Livius* 8. *Lib.* Nofter duorum eventus oftendat. The fecond is of u-
niverfall and particular. 3. *Orat.* Voluntati
veftrum omnium parui (Alfo it might have
beene veftræ for veftrum) *Brutus Cicer.* Qui
veftris paucorum refpondent laudibus. The
third is of unius, folius, ipfius. *Cic.* Mea unius opera. *Att.* Solius enim meum pecca-
tum corrigi non poteft. *Pro. Mur.* Conjectu-
ram de tuo ipfius ftudio facillimè ceperis.

The

The fourth is of verbals. *Ep.* Quocunq; tempore mihi potestas præsentis tui fuerit. Notwithstanding *Cato* writing to *Cicero* sayth, libenter facio vt tuam virtutem, innocentiam, diligentiam cognitam, in maximis rebus, domi togati, armati foris, pari industria administrari gaudeam. here togati hath the like case vnto the verball. But with much more libertie. 2. *Phil.* Tuum hominis simplicis pectus vidimus.

Thirdly. The gerund in *di*, is as it were the genitive case of a subiect. 1. *Off.* Pueris non omnem licentiam ludendi damus. For the which sometimes the infinite perpetuall is added. 2. *Orat.* Tempus esset jam de ordine argumentorum dicere. *Cæs.* 7. Consilium ceperunt ex oppido profugere.

The *second rection of a substantive* remayneth to be spoken of.

The substantive of the subiect or the whole, serveth to the genitive or the ablative of the adiunct or the part, with an adiective of praise or dispraise 6. *Ep.* Accipies hospitem non multi cibi, sed multi, joci. *Ter. And.* Virgo, sparso ore, adunco naso.

Opus, beeing a worde of case, and a substantive, governeth an ablative case. 9. *Ep.* Authoritate tua nobis opus est, & consilio, & gratia. *Att.* Sed opus fuit Hircio convento. *Sal.* priusquam incipias, consulto, & ubi consulueris,

sulueris, maturè facto opus est. From which
construction do arise these phrases of *Terence.*
Opus dictu, opus factu . And also of *Cicero,* o-
pus scitu.

Cap. 2.
Of an Adiective.

THe *rection* of an adiective is divers: and it
is to be seene for the most part in *quantity,*
and in *quality:* in *quantitie,* of degree, partition,
and plenty.

The *comparative degree* doth governe an ablative case, and that when mention is made of
two, or of very many beeing of divers natures:
that is, when the substantive of degree is not
contayned in the case of rection or government
Horat . Vilius argentum est auro, virtutibus
aurum . That is to say, gold is more excellent
then silver, and vertues then gold.

The *superlative degree* doth governe a genitive case plurall, and that when mention is
made of manye , which are of one and the
selfe same nature : that is to saye , when the
substantive of degree is contained in the case
of rection. *In Brn.* Crassus eloquentium juris-
peritissimus , jurisperitorum eloquentissimus Scævola.

A *partitive adiective* doth governe a genitive
case. *Sal. Iug.* Quis est omnium his moribus?

VVhich sig-
nifieth the
part.

H 2. *Div.*

2. *Div*.utrum igitur eorum accidiffet, verum
oraculum fuiffet.4.*Ep*.Nigidio uni omnium
doctiffimo. Sometime the nominatiue cafe
is ufed for the genitiue cafe of partition. *Liv.*
lib. 41.Periti religionum iùrifque publici,
quando duodenarij Coff. eius anni alter
morbo, alter ferro perijffet,fuffectum Conf.
negabant comitia habere poffe.

An adiectiue of plentie or fcarfenes, doth gouerne a Genitiue or an Ablatiue cafe: as Ple-
nus bonorum & bonis. 2. *Frat*. Literæ refer-
tæ omni officio. Vacuum laboris, & labore.
Inane prudentia,& prudentiæ. Oratione locuples. Inops verborum & verbis. Orbus
omnibus rebus.

Now followeth the *rection* of *qualitie,in affinitie,commoditie,and* defire.

An adiectiue of affinitie, or *of the contrarye,*
doth gouerne a Genitiue or a datiue cafe. *Pro.*
Syl.Affinis fufpicionis & fufpicioni. So ami-
cus,inimicus,alienus,fimilis,par,communis,
proprius. 1. *Orat*. Finitimus oratori. 3. *Off*.
Voluptas contraria honeftati.

An adiectiue of commoditie, or *of the contrarie,*
doth gouerne a datiue cafe: as alicui commo-
dum,incommodum,accommodatum,utile,
inutile, infeftum, infenfum, moleftum, gra-
tum, ingratum, grave, jucundum, injucun-
dum,charum,dulce.

An

An adiective of desire, doth governe a genitive case, but after divers sorts. first, that which hath an active apparance. *Att.* Amantissimus utriusque nostrum. 2. *Orat.* Dispiciens sui. But *pro Deiot.* Audiens dicto esset huic ordini.

Secondly, which hath an apparance of a passive. 6. *Phil.* Consultus juris, Insuetus contumeliæ. So peritus and imperitus rerum.

Thirdly, in *dus*, 1. *Orat.* Laudis cupidus, avidus victoriæ. So providus and improvidus rerum.

Fourthly, in *osus, ius, tus.* Studiosus doctrinarum, Rerum coscij, Gnarus reipublicæ, Ignarus fortunarum suarum. *Quint. lib.* 8. *cap.* 4. Securus tam parvæ observationis. To conclude, others ending after a divers sort, have also this construction. *Pro. Flacc.* Rerum omnium rudis. *Ep.* 6. memores virtutis: Immemor mandati. 1. *Frat.* Dignitatis superstes. Prudens, & imprudens rerum, voluptatis particeps vel expers: so compos and impos: also expers fama & fortunis. *Salust.* But we use dignus laudis and laude. An adiective of that sort doth oftentimes take a perpetuall infinite or a participiall in *di*, for the genitive case of a noune. 1. *Cæs.* 11. paratus omnia perpeti. *In Ep.* Cupidus satisfaciendi. 3. *Off.* Peritus definiendi.

Also certaine adiectives doe governe the first
supine. 1.*Cat.*Optimum factu.*De Fato.*Facile
intellectu.*Terent. Adelph.*Natu maximus.*Pro
Plancio.*O rem tum auditu crudelem, tum visu nefariam.

Cap. 3.

Of the rection of a verb active.

Hitherto we have spoken of the *rection* of a
noune, there followeth the *rection* of a
verbe . First of a finite verbe , and that personall : whereby sometimes a noune, and sometime a verb is governed.

The *rection* of a finte verbe personall, whereby a noune is governed , is eyther of the firste
kinde, or of the second. There is but one onely
rule of the first rection.

A *verb active* doth governe after him an accusative case. *In Ep.* Fortem virum tibi commendo: but, Marco Tullio igni & aqua inter-
dicatur, is *Cicero* his phrase *pro Dom.* And Sa-
tage rerum tuarum, sayd *Terence in Heaut.*

A *verbe passive* doth governe an ablative case.
as *Horat.*Fortes creantur fortibus. But this
rection is very rare or seldome without a preposition . The dative is here sometimes used
for the ablative case. *Ad. Lent.*Neque senatui,
neque populo, neque cuiquam bono proba-
                                        tur.

tur. Neuters and Deponents do governe no case of them-selues, as sedeo, loquor: notwith-standing they doe sometime * imitate the recti- Or follow on of a verbe actiue. 2. *Fin.* Hæc cum loqueris, nos Varrones stupemus. 2. *Agr.* Currere cur-sum, *In Ep.* Gaudere gaudium, *In Top.* Seruire seruitutem. 3. *Orat.* Ceram ac crocum olere. So infinite others, as aliquem mirari, ulcisci: odorari ingressus : conqueri, non lamentari fortunam. But utor, vescor, fungor, fruor, potior, do governe an ablatiue case. It is also sayd, potiri rerum, *Planc.* Quæ patriæ benefi-cia meminerunt: and also, memini actionum, *in Ep.* So three Deponents do governe a geni-tiue or an accusatiue case, to wit, obliuiscor, reminiscor, recordor.

And this is the first kind of *rection*. The se-cond is, when as beside this former case an o-ther case is gouerned: and that either simple, or diuers: as the Datiue, the Accusatiue, and the Ablatiue.

GAP 4.

Of the rection of a verb of ac-quisition.

A Verbe by the force of *acquisition*, doth go-verne a Datiue case. *Hor.* 3, *Epist.* Quid

3   mihi

mihi Celfus agit ? *Cic. in Pifo.* Is mihi etiam
gloriabitur. *Ad Treb.* Ecce tibi Pompejus.
Ter. Suo fibi hunc jugulo gladio. **But verye
manye Uerbes do governe the fame cafe, by a
certaine germane nature or neare affinitie.**

First: verbes of comparifon. 1. *Off.* Se illis fere
æquarunt. *In Brut.* Vt conferamus parva ma-
gnis. *Ter. Heau.* Homo homini quid præ-
ftat, Cæteris excellere: fo antecellere, antece-
dere : but *pro Cor,* there is alfo, Cæteros ante-
cellis, &c.

Secondly, verbes of giving, and the contrary. 2.
Verr. Quæ victores civitatibus ficulis aut dederunt aut reddiderunt. 4. *Verr.* Scribitur
Heraclio dica. 6. *Att.* Mitte mihi obviam literas. *Pro Marc.* Operibus tuis diuturnitas
detrahet. *Att.* Dubitationem mihi tolles. *In
Brut.* Collegæ fuo imperium abrogavit.

*Thirdly, verbes of commaunding, ferving, fhew-
ing or declaring, and promifing. De Amic.* Cupiditatibus, quibus cæteri ferviunt, imperare.
5. *Ep.* Tibi non fignificandum folum, fed de-
clarandum. *Pro Cæl.* Promitto hoc vobis, reipub. fpondeo. 5. *Ep.* Profiteri alicui & polliceri
ri ftudium fuum. 7. *Att.* Tempori parcamus.

Fourthlie, verbes of refifting, and the contrarie.
Pro Rab. Repugnare & refiftere crudelitati.
Pro Comædo. Hominib. irafci & fuccenfere. 4.
Att. Valde mihi arriferat. *Pro Lig.* Cujus ego
induftriæ gloriæque faveo . **So affentio, and**
moze

moꝛe often aſſentior.

*Fifthly, thoſe verbes which ſometimes are taken
imperſonally,*haue this rection of the datiue caſe
3.*Frat.*Nihil ei reſtabat.5.*Fin.* Quod ipſis ſu-
perat. 7. *Ep.*Conſiſtat tibi fructus otij tui.5.
*Tuſcul.*peccare licet nemini. Pro *Clu.* Qui ſibi
non liquere dixerunt. *In Brut.* Dolet mihi.
And thoſe datiue caſes which are put foꝛ accuſatiue caſes,do ſeeme to be of this kind. Qui ſe
patriæ, & ſuis civibus, qui laudi,qui gloriæ,
non qui ſomno,convivijs & delectationi natos arbitrentur.And this is the rection of the
Datiue caſe.

Cap. 5.

Of the rection of verbes of asking
or intreating.

Certaine *verbes of asking* doe goberne an o-
ther accuſatiue caſe. *Ter,* Illud te oro. *I-
dem.*Sine te hoc exorem. So,obſecro,rogo,
flagito, and ſuch like berbes of demaund. Alſo
moneo,conſulo,celo,doceo,*in Orat,*Qui nos
nihil celat : but celo tibi rem,celo te de hac
re,is alſo uſed.*In* P*ſſ.*Quid te aſine literas doceam : ſo dedoceo. Alſo doceo te de re. But
there remayneth a dubble caſe alſo in the paſ-
ſiue foꝛme:as,per Legatos cuncta edocetur.

Of the rection of verbes of plenty
and of price.

A *Verbe of plenty and of price*, doth gouerne an
Ablatiue case. Of plenty oz the contrary:
as 6. *Verr.* Complere aliquem coronis & floribus. 2. *Phil.* Saturare se sanguine. 1. *Orat.*
Abundare doctrina. 2. *Fin.* Affluere volupta-
tibus. Apollonium omni argento spoliasti.
So exinanire, vacuare, But *Cicero* hath sayde,
artis indigere; and *Terence*, Tui carendum e-
rat. Uerbes of pzice : as *Pro Rabir.* Mercari
magno pretio. *Pro Amer.* Tanto pretio mercari, *Terence in Andria.* Vix drachmis obsona-
tus est decem. 5. *Verr.* Tritici modium quater-
nis sestertijs æstimasset. From whence doth
spzing this construction, Valere authoritate,
ingenio. Notwithstanding *Varro* sayde. De-
nos æris valebant. And certaine nounes are
gouerned in the genitiue case, as quanti, tanti, magni, pluris, maximi, plurimi, parvi, minoris, minimi, æqui, boni, flocci, nihili, nauci, pili, assis, teruntij. Depactus est tantidem, quanti fidem suam fecit. *Brut.* *Cic.* Nihil tanti fuit. 1. *Acad.* Alia pluris æsti-
manda, alia minoris. 3. *Fin.* Plurimi æsti-
mandum. 1. *Ep.* A me minimi putaban-
tur. Also this Phzase following is in *Terence*:
Quid

Quid agas, niſi ut te redimas quâ queas mi-
nimo? ſi nequeas paullulo, at quanti queas.
Plautus. facitis magni. *Ter. And.* Te ſemper
maximi feci, 7. *Att.* Iſtud æqui bonique facit:
ſo boni conſulere. *Pro Arch.* Pericula parvi eſſe ducêda, but magno æſtimare, conſequi vo-
luptates, non modò parvo ſed ferme nihilo,
are *Ciceroes phꝛaſes. Att.* Remp. flocci non facere. 3. *Fin.* Nihili facio. But foꝛ nihilo putare
is oftentimes uſed. Habere, ducere, videri. 1.
Div. Non habeo denique nauci Marſum au-
gurem: ſo, ne pili, neaſsis facere.

Cap. 7.

Of the rection of a verbe Iudiciall.

And this is the ſecond kinde of the rection of a
ſimple caſe. There followeth the rection of
the variable caſe in a iudiciall verbe, & a verbe
ſubſtantiue.

A judiciall verbe governeth a genitive, or an
ablative caſe: as verbes of accuſing, and of ab-
ſolving. 2. *Finib.* Eam tanquam capitis accu-
et. 3. *Ver.* Suis eum certis proprijſq; crimi-
nibus accuſabo. pro *Dejotaro.* Capitis arceſ-
ſere. pro *Cel.* Ambitus crimine accerſere. 3.
Ver. Verrem inſimulat avaritiæ & audaciæ.
So theſe phꝛaſes followyng, arguere rei capi-
talis, arguere crimine, ſcelere alligare, ſcelere
è aſtringere, are uſed of *Cicero.* Damnari ma-
jeſtatis,

jeſtatis,furti,injuriarum, ambitus,cædis,ſce-
lerum,imprudentiæ.Inertiæ condénare.But
there is alſo,crimine códénare,multare morte,exilio,multa,pecunia.Plecti capite,culpa.2
*Phil.*Convincere inhumanitatis & amentiæ.2
2.*Verr.*Abſolvere improbitatis.*Pro Clu.* ma-
jeſtatis,2.*Verr.*Crimine liberare.*Liv.lib.* 51,
Nec liberavit ejus culpæ regé:*Idé.*5.*lib.* Quin
ſine mora voti liberaretur.But notwithſtanding as *Valla* doth teach,you ſhal onely ſay,vtro
accuſatus es furti an cædis?not utrius: and in
the like caſe,utroq; neutro,ambobus.

C A P. 8.

Of the rection of a verbe ſubſtantive.

A *Verbe ſubſtantive, or a verbe which obtaineth
the force of a verbe ſubſtantive, doth governe
after it a nominative caſe,taken from the ſame:* as
Tullius eſt Romanus:Tullius cognominatus
eſt Cicero.14.*Ep.*Beatiſsimi viveremus.That
which followeth is particular or proper to the
infinitive mood.1.*Tuſc.*Licuit otioſo eſſe The-
miſtocli . *Brutus Ciceroni:* ut optimè meritis
de republica liceat eſſe ſalvis. 1. *Catil.* Cupio
me eſſe clementem.

*But if the caſe be of a poſſeſſor,it ſhall be put in the
genitive caſe,*2.*Ep.*Iam me Pompeji totum eſſe ſcis . *pro Manil.* Erit igitur humanitatis ve-
ſtræ.3.*Off.*Emere denario quod ſit mille de-
narium.

narium. But fo2 thefe genitiues mei, tui, sui.
&c. are put thefe poffeffiues meum, tuum, suú,
noftrum veftrum: *Pro Balb.* Non enim eft meum cótra aliquem dicere : Noftrum eft intel-
ligere. The fame verbe if it be ufed fo2 habeo,
voth gouerne a vatiue cafe, as. 1. *Eneid.*

  Sunt mihi bis septé præftáti corpore nymphæ. To the which thefe o2ations feeme to be-
long wherein gerundes vo follow. *Fam.* 5. Tué-
da tibi ut fit gravitas , & conftantiæ feruien-
dú. 1. *de Or.* Gerendus eft tibi mos adolefcé-
tibus *Craffe.* But this verbe eft, ferving fo2 afferre, will haue a vouble vatiue cafe. 2. *Ep.* ut
sempiternæ laudi tibi fit ifte tribunatus ex-
opto, The paffiue participle of the future téfe,
which Grammarians haue fayned to be in dus,
is circumfcribed of the infinite future of the
verbe fubftantiue fore, and the participle perfectly paft. *Cicero.* Quo in genere fperare vi-
deor Scipionis amicitiam & Lælij notam po-
fteritati fore. *Cef.* 1. *Lib.* Commiffum cum e-
quitatu prælium fore videbatur.

Cap. 9.

Of the rection of verbes
of deliberation.

Hitherto *we haue spoken of the rection of a finite verbe personall , whereby a noune is gouerned of a verbe. There remayneth that rection*

on whereby a verbe is governed of a verbe : as is used in verbes of deliberation and motion.

A verbe deliberative,doth governe a perpetuall infinite: as,audeo,habeo,incipio, opto,soleo, statuo,scio,volo,maturo, desisto, debeo, cupio,paro,possum,propero: aggredior, molior,conor : licet,delectat, decet,tædet, piget, pænitet. Also verbes of tense:as video, audio, *6.Att.*Obsecras ne obliviscar vigilare,*6.Ver.* hoc memini te dicere. 1 . *de Leg* , juri studere te memini.1.*Attic.*De commitijs tibi me permisisse memini:*pra. Mil.*Meminit etiã sibi voce præconis modo defuisse. This *Anomalie* of tenses,of the present for the pretertense,hath here growne into use. Sometime the verbe deliberative it selfe is concealed. 5.*Ver.* Ridere convivæ, cachinnari ipse Apronius . for here is understoode cæperunt,& cæpit.Contrariwise sometime the infinite verbe is concealed . *Teren.Eun.*Et fidibus scire , pretium sperans.*In. Brut.*Non enim tam præclarum est scire Latinè,quam turpe nescire.

Cap. 10.

Of the rection of a verbe of motion.

A Verbe *of moving to a place,doth governe the second supine which wanteth both gender & number.*3.*Orat.* Imus-ne sessum?etsi admonitum venimus te,non flagitatum. Where that

peri-

periphrasis of the infinite future perpetuall of the active voyce, wherof I spake but a litle before. *Plaut. Mil.* credo te facilè impetratum ire, and also of the passive voyce. 15. *Att.* Brutum visum iri á me puto. *Att.* Multò firmius acta tyrāni comprobatum iri. *Ter. And.* Postquam audierat non datum iri filio uxorem suo: Sometyme here also the perpetuall infinite is governed in stead of the supine. *Plau. Pen.* Venerat autem petere. *Ter.* Eamus videre. But this is more seldome. A verbe of moving from a place doth sometime governe the first supine. *Plau.* Obsonatu redeo. *Cato.* Cubitu resurgo.

CAP. II.

Of the rection of an infinite verbe, and a verbe impersonall.

WE have already spoken of the rection of a finite verbe personall, now it is tyme to speake of the rection of a verbe infinite and impersonall.

A perpetuall infinite verb personall, doth governe an accusative case before him. *Ter.* Meum natum rumor est amare. And the same infinite verbe doth governe after it the case of his finite verbe *Ter.* Quapropter teipsum purgare ipsis coram placabilius est. Both the last gerund and the last supine taken for the most part impersonally,

nally doe also governe the case of their finite
verbe. *Plaut*. aliqua consilia reperiendum est.
Varro. colligendū eas in vas aliquod. But you
shall rather speake that by the gerundive (although the other be used amongest the Greci-
ans) Aliqua consilia reperienda, colligendæ
in vas aliquod. Notwithstandyng in verbes
neuters and deponentes it shall be of force: Ad
Lentulum temporibus assentiendum. *Pro Se-*
stio. Reipub. consulendum, dignitati servien-
dum. 7. *Att*. An misero bello esset utendum.
And the second supine is often in like construction. 1. *Att*. Huic quoque rei subventum est.
Eius orationi reclamatū est. For it hath onely the active rection with verbs of moouing to
a place. *Teren. And*. Cur te is perditum? Missa
est ancilla illico obstetricem accersitum.
Which hath also place in the passive oration.
Ibidem. Postquam audierat non datum iri
filio uxorem suo. Moreouer the passive rection may be added. 15. *Att*. Brutum visum iri à
me puto.

Cap. 12.

Of the rection of an impersonall.

THe rection of certaine impersonals is proper. Refert and interest, *signifing commo-*
ditie or dutie, do governe a genitive case. *Sal*. Illorum retulisse videretur. *Pro Dom*. Reipublicæ
interesse

interesse putavi.3. *Epist*. Vtriusq; nostrum interest,ejus,ipsius,illius,refert,interest.Except
seven genitive cases,mei,tui,sui,nostri, vestri,
nostrum , & vestrum : for which the possessives are used:as refert &interest mea,tua,sua,
nostra,vestra:also cvja. *Pro Mu*. Ea cædes po-
tissimùm crimini datur ei,cuja interfuit,non
ei cuja nihil interfuit.

*Also refert and interest , doe admit these geni-
tive cases of price and estimation:* tanti , quanti,
magni , parvi. In the rest they have more often, multum , plus , plurimum , magis , minus, parum, paululum , pauxillulum , nihil,
aliquid.

Five impersonals, to wit . Miseret, miserescit,
or miseretur,tædet,piget, pœnitet, & pudet,
*do governe an accusative case of the thing , with a
genitive case of the sufferer Ter. Heau*. Menede-
mi vicem miseret me. *Ibidem* . Me tuarum
misertum est fortunarum. *Ibidem* . Te nunc
inopis miserescat mei. *Pro Ligar* . Cavete
fratrum pro fratris salute precantium vòs
misereatur. *2. Att*. Prorsus nos vitæ tædet.
Pro Dom. Me non solùm piget stultitiæ meæ,
sed etiam pudet. *Teren. Phor*. Omnes nostri-
met nos pœnitet. *1. Verr*. Sunt homines
quos libidinis & infamiæ suæ neque pudeat
neque tædeat.

CAP.

CAP. 13,

Of the rection of adverbes.

HItherto we have spoken of the rection of
wordes of number. The rection of adverbes
shall follow, which is very variable.

Derivatives doe keepe the case of their primiti-
ves. 10. *Att.* Nihilo minus, *In Brut.* Omnium
elegátissimè. Of which sort are those that follow . Mihi similiter , Tibi æqualiter , Naturæ
convenienter & congruenter.

Adverbes of place do governe a genitive case of
redundance, but notwithstanding very usuall, 5. *Att.*
Vbi terrarum esses, 2. *Phil.* Vbicunque terrarum. 6. *Att.* Tu autem abes longe gentium. 2.
Cat, ubinam gentium? *Plautus Ru.* Quovis gé-
tium ? *idem,* unde gentium ? also somewhat o-
therwise is that. 9. *Att.* At quàm honesta, quà
expedita tua consilia , quà itineris , quà navi-
gationis , quà congressus, sermonisque cum
Cæsare ? That is , partly concerning the iour-
ney, and partly concerning the navigation. 11.
Att. Quoad ejus fieri poterit.

Adverbes of time, as pridie. *i.* præcedenti die,
postridie, *i.* postero die , have a threefold construction. 11. *Att.* Illam sententiam pridie e-
jus diei fregeramus. *Cæsar .* 1 . Postridie ejus
diei. 8. *Epist.* Postridie absolutionis . Here is
the genitive case. 7. *Phil.* Qui cum pridie fre-
quentes essetis assensi, postridie ad spem estis
                   inanem

inanem pacis devoluti. Here the case of tyme
is concealed, being expressed before. *Att.* Pridie
compitalia, Pridie nonas, Pridie calendas. In
these the accusative case is ioyned: where not=
withstandyng Grammarians doe understand
ante, Postridie Idus. Postridie ludos. Also in
the accusative cases following they thinke post
to be concealed. *De Amicit.* Pridie quàm excessit è vita. 12. *Epist.* usque Postridie intelle-
xi cùm a vobis discessi. *ad Attic.* usq; ad pridie calendas.

Adverbes of quantitie, as parum and satis,
do governe a genitive case. *Plautus.* Parum malæ
rei. *Teren. And.* Pro peccato magno paulum
supplicij satis est patri, Agelli hîc sub vrbe est
paululum. *Teren. Phorm.* Satis iam verborum
est. So tantum, quantum, multi, will in like
maner have a genitive case.

En, ecce, & O, *doe governe a nominative or an
accusative.* 13. *Epist.* En hic ille est. *Plautus in
Amph.* En tectum, en tegulas, en obductas
fores, en ludificatum herum. 14. *ad Att.* Ecce autem Antonius. 2. *de Fin.* Ecce miserum
hominem. *Pro Cæl.* O consuetudo peccandi.
3. *Phil.* O præclarum custodem ovium, vt ajunt, lupum.

Hei, *is either without case, or els governeth a
dative or a vocative case.* *Terent. In And.* Hei
vereor. *Cic.* Hei mihi. *Terent. in Eun.* Hei noster, laudo.

I   Hei,

Heu,*doth governe a dative, an accusative, and a vocative case.* Plaut. heu misero mihi. *Virg.* heu fuge nate dea.*In Tus.* Heu me infelicem.

Heus,*doth governe a vocative case.* Terent. *in* Heaut.Heus,Heus Syre.

Væ, *doth governe a dative case* Terent. væ capiti tuo.

Pro, *doth governe an accusative and vocative case.*5. *Tusc.* Prò deum atq; hominum fidem. *Terent.In Adelp.*Prô sancte Iupiter.

C A P. 14.

Of the rection of prepositions which governe an accusative case.

PRepositions have a native signification of place: but they do often serve to times, persons,and thynges. Amongest these some do governe one case onely,and some two cases.These which doe governe but one case, doe either governe the accusative, or els the ablative alone. There are one and thirtie prepositions which governe the accusative case.

Intra, extra: *Pro.Cel.* Ingrediens intra finem hujus loci. *in Verr.* Intra decem annos. 6. *Epist.* Intra legem. *Teren.in Phorm.* extra ostium. *Pro Syl.* extra conjurationem, jocum,modū,culpam.7. *Epist.* Extra ducem, paucosque.

Apud,penes, apud igné assidere: apud Senatum.

natũ. 2. *Att*. Apud me, 4. *Att*. Apud Pompejum. After which sort you shall rather speake, then, apud domum meam, tuam, Pompeji: although it be the same. Penes scenam exercitatus. *Pro. Dom*. penes Censorem iudicium Senatus de dignitate majores esse voluerunt

Secus, secundum. *Plin. Lib*. 10. *Cap*. 24. Nascitur secus fluvios. 16. *Attic*. Iter secundum mare superum faciunt. 2. *Off*. Proximè & secundum deos, homines hominibus maximè utiles. *Cice*. 1. *de Orat*. Secundum hunc diem. 1. *Verr*. Secundũ binos ludos. 4. *Verr*. De absente secundum præsentem judicare. But it is often understoode. *pro Am*. duo filij id ætatis. *Varro*. Ab id genus alijs: but especially in the Poete, as

Os humer osq; Deo similis. - - -

Iuxta, prope. *Plaut*. Iuxta te sum. Iuxta Deos, id est, gratia deorum. Iuxta libertatem. 1. secundum. Prope montes. 1. *Epist*. prope cal. Sextiles.

Ante, post, pone: as ante focum. 14. *Epist*. ante oculos. 8. *ad Attic*. Quem ante me diligo. 2. *De Invent*. Multò ante lucem surrexit. 9. *Attic*. Post diem quartum. *pro Balbo*. Post genus hominum natum. 11. *in Phil*. Post homines natos. *Piso*. Post hominum memoriam. *Cæs*. 7. Post tergum. Pone castra. *De univers*. Pone quos.

Cis, citra, præter. Cis is commonly added,

to the names of mountaines and rivers. 7. *Att.*
Quoad hostis cis Euphratem fuit. 3. *Ep.* Cis
Taurum. *Cæſ.* 6. Citra Rhenum. Citra pulve-
ris jactum. *i.* ſine. *Liv.lib.* 40. Præter mœnia
fluere. So præter ripam, oculos. Præter cæteros divinare. Præter expectationem, fidem,
modum, naturam, conſuetudinem. 7. *Attic.*
Omnes præter eum de quo egimus.

Vltra, trans. 9. *Att.* ultra Salianā villam eſt.
4. *Tuſc.* ultra modum regredi. 12. *Att.* Cogi-
to interim trans Tyberim hortos aliquos pa-
rare. *Pro Mil.* trans ripam inſpicere. This prepoſition in compoſition doth retayne moſt commonly his caſe. 2. *Nat.* Grues maria tranſmit-
tunt. *Cæſ.* 1. Flumen Anoxā exercitum tradu-
cere maturavit. *Idem.* 4. Exercitū modó Rhenum tranſportaret.

Inter. 1. *Leg.* uſucapionem duodecim ta-
bulæ inter quinque pedes eſſe voluerunt. 7.
Verr. Inter manus. 3. *Frat.* valent pueri, ſtudi-
oſè diſcunt, & nos & inter ſe amant. 1. *de Div.*
Noſque inter nos complexos narrabat. But
the other caſe is moꝛe often concealed. 2. *de O-*
rat. Qui cum inter ſe, ut ipſorum uſus ferebat, amiciſſimè conſalutaſſent. From hence
commeth this conſtruction alſo. Inter nos tot
unus inuentus. *Virg.* 9. *Eccl.* Inter agendum.
id eſt, dum agis. *Plaut. in Ciſtel.* Sed inter rem
agendam. But notwithſtanding you ſhall rather ſpeake it by the noune. 3. *Frat.* Hoc inter
cœnam

cœnam Tyroni dictavi. 7. *Ep.* Illuseras heri inter scyphos. *Ter, in Eun.* Inter vias. Sometime this is a iudiciall word. 2. *Phil.* Eos inter sicarios defensurus, After which sort the lawyers say, inter reos deferre.

Inter, with a relatiue reciprocatiue and a demonstratiue, hath a proper agreement beside his case. For a nominatiue or an accusatiue going before, there is onely added a reciprocatiue. 3. *Offic.* Quòd inter se omnes partes quodam lepore consentiunt. *Ibidem.* Damonem & Pythiam Pithagoreos ferunt hoc animo inter se fuisse. But a genitiue, datiue, or ablatiue going before, a demonstratiue may be added for a reciprocatiue. *Ter. In Adel.* Communia esse amicorum inter se omnia. *In Bruto.* Ipsorum inter ipsos concessu. *In Phil.* Quorum suum quondam inter ipsos odium meministis. 2. *Att.* Istorū inter istos dissentio. 1. *Offic.* Multa sunt civibus inter se communia. *Ibidem.* Latissimè patés hominibus inter ipsos societas hæc est. *Quint. lib. 6, cap.* 2. A doctis inter ipsos etiam mutuo reprehensa. It might also haue bene sayd, a doctis inter se.

Erga and contra, haue almost lost their natiue signification of place, and haue taken vnto them the signification of good will or duty, and hatred. 1. *Epist.* Ego omni officio ac potius pietate erga te, cæteris satisfacio omnibus. *Pro R. Com.* Repugnare et resistere contra verita-

3

veritatem.2.*Phil,*Homo diſertus non intelli-
git eum quem contradicit, laudari à ſe, eos
apud quos dicit, vituperari. *Caeſ. 7.* Contra
omnium expectationem. So contra opinio-
nem,ſpem,legem,naturam,officium.

Ad, uſque. *De Sen.* ad focum ſedere. So
ad judices, patres. Quirites, populum. 1
Cat. ad M. Leccam te habitare velle dixiſti.
Terent. Ad dexteram, ad ſiniſtram. 4. *Attic.*
Ad quid laboramus res Romanas? *Pro Pomp.*
Locus ad agendum ampliſſimus.2. *Orat.* Li-
cinium ſervum ſibi Gracchus habuit ad ma-
num. Alſo, Ad arbitrum ſcribere, ad nor-
mam & ſimilitudinem dirigere, ad ſpeciem
adumbrare,ad aſpectum praeclarus. 1.*de Div.*
Mirari licet quae ſunt animadverſa a medi-
cis herbarum genera,quae radicum, ad mor-
ſus beſtiarum, ad oculorum morbos. 1 . *de
Div.*ad lucem dormire .*in Somn*.ad multam
noctem vigilare.2.*Phil.*Ad veſperum perpo-
tare.12.*Attic.* Ad decem annos, uſque ado-
leſcentiâ meam proceſſit aerate. Hîc,à Brunduſio uſque Romam perpetuum agmen vi-
derem. But often tymes it is compounded
with ad,*Teren.And.*Verberibus caeſum uſque
ad necem.

Verſus is alwayes put after the word he governeth in compoſition: and *adverſus,* beyng
compounded thereof, is put before: *Plautus.*
Ego portum verſus pergam, Adverſus & ad-
ver-

versum. *Cicero.* 1. *Off.* sunt autem quædam of-
ficia etiam adversus eos servanda, à quibus
injuriam acceperis. Pietas est justitia adversus deos. But *Sal.* Animadvertit ad se fugam
versus fieri. Here the partes of the compounde
are separated.

Ob. *pro Posth.* Ob oculos versari. *Pro Marc.*
Ob delictum pœnas dij expetunt. Sometime
it is concealed. *Terent. in Eun.* Nunc id pro-
deo, ut conveniam Parmenonem.

Per, propter. Per totam caveam ire. 5.
Verr. Per beneficium & gratiam aliquid
concedere. *Pro Dom.* In bona fortunasque
locupletum, per causam inopum atque im-
peritorum, repentinos impetus comparare,
id est, per speciem. From hence also is that,
Aliquot jam per annos. So per eos dies. 2.
De *Inv.* Propter Lacedæmonem fluit. 4. *Verr.*
Propter ædem Vulcani. 1. *Epist.* Propter tuum in me amorem.

Infra, supra. 2. *de Nat.* Infra Saturnum jovis
stella. *Post Red.* Infra omnes mortuos aman-
dari. *In Somn.* Supra Lunam sunt omnia æter-
na. *Ad Octav.* supra ætatem, consuetudinem,
supra etiam mortalitatem.

Circa, circum, circiter. 2. *Agr.* circa Capuam. Circa curam valetudinis tuæ, circa eum
mensem.

Circum. 2. *Verr.* Cursare circum tribus, versari circum axim cœli.

Circiter. *Plaut*. *Cift*. Loca hæc circiter excidit mihi. Hereof commeth Circiter meridiem.

CAP. 15.

Of the rection of prepositions governing an ablative case.

There are. 14. prepositions which governe an ablative case.

Præ. *Liv. Lib*. 1. Præ se armentum agens, From hence commeth this construction, præ nobis beatus. *In Brut*. Illos Atticos præ se penè agrestes putat, *pro*. *Rab*. præ me sero. 9. *Attic*. præ lacrymis.

Pro. 2. *Phil*. pro æde jovis Statoris. 3. *de Orat*. pro omnibus. *pro Arch*. Se gerere pro cive. Pro dignitate, pro consuetudine.

Cum. *Cic*. *Cum* potestate esse.

Sine: Sine auro ornata. *Terent*. Imperium sine fine.

Coram, palam. *In Pif*. coram genere meo. *Liv. lib*. 6. Palam Populo.

Tenus is alwayes put after the worde which it governeth. *Pro*. *Deit*. Tauro tenus. *Liv*. 26. umbilico tenus. 1. *Leg*. verbo tenus. And it doth governe a genitive case plurall signifiing double thynges, or wantyng the singular number: as *Quintil*. 12. Aurium tenus. *Virg*. Crurum tenus. *In Epist*. Cumarum tenus. Onely this preposition governeth

neth a genitiue case.

De,ex,e,abs, absque, and a, are also Prepoſitions ſignifying place. But they doe rather ſhew a cauſe, and they doe runne through the greateſt part of *Syntax*, or conſtruction of Adiectiues and Uerbes expounded before, & they doe very much helpe and adorne it. De,ex,and ab,are put before all other letters : e and a:are onely put before conſonants. De,ex,and e,doe ſhew the matter. Ciceronis liber de Officijs, De Oratore,and ſuch like titles of books.*Att.* De lingua latina ſecuri res animi. Alſo it is uſed in ſome, in which it was not or hath not beene before.*Pro Lig.*De quibuſdam reminiſcentem recordari, Deferre de repetundis,de ambitu damnari, Accuſare de negligentia, de veneficijs, are *Ciceroes* phraſes againſt the *analogy* of iudicials, De repetundis pecunijs,de majeſtate.

Ex.ſtatua ex æra facta,Simulacrum ex ære, poculum ex auro,are *Ciceroes* phraſes.9.*Epiſt.* Ex pedibus laborare.Sometimes it is all one in ſence with the prepoſition ſecundùm : as in *Adelph.*Ex æquo & bono. *Pro Amerino.* Ex ſua natura cæteros fugere.It ſerueth for comparison and partition 4.*Fin.*Primi ex omnibus Philoſophis.3.*Att.*unus ex omnibus amicis. *Pro Cluent.*Paucos ex multis ad ignominiam ſortiri.*Cæſ.*1.unos ex omnibus Sequanos nihil earum rerum facere.*Pro Arch.*ut primùm

ex

ex pueris excessit.9. *Att.*Ex ea die venti sep-
tentriones fuere.

E:4.*Acad.* E saxo sculptus,aut ebore dola-
tus.2.*Tusc.*Laborare è renibus ، 1.*Phil.* Lan-
guere è via.*De Fin.* Húc statū corporis expe-
tit qui est è natura maximè.&o è republica.

Ab.*Terent.*.*And.* Otiosus ab animo،1.*Att.*
Inops ab amicis.

Abs,is onelye put before t and q : *Terent.in
Phormi.*Abij abs te.*Idem Adelph.*Abs quivis
homine.

Absque:*Plaut.*Absque te si fuissem hodie.

A:*in Epist.*، Aliud à libertate communi، *In
Luc.*à te totus diversus، Vacuus à suspicione،
*Post Red.*Nudus a propinquis9.*Epist.* Alienus
à dignitate. Qui erant à Platone,that is,Pla-
tonici vel Platonis discipuli، These prepositions beeing ioyned unto verbes passives, and to
those verbes which be of that kind,do expresse
an agent cause.*Quint.li.*12.*Ca.*1.Fabricius respondit à cive se spoliari malle,quàm ab ho-
ste vænire.*Idem lib.*9.*cap.*2. An ab eo fustibus
vapulasset.10. *Epist.* Cùm ei magnum convi-
cium fieret cun&o à Senatu. *Pro Milon.* Bea-
tos esse quibus ea res honori fuerit à suis ci-
vibus،

Verbes of desiring, of receaving , and of re-
mooving,doe imitate the same construction.6.
*Att.*Binas à te accepi literas. 4.*Acad.*Cùm à
veris falsa non distent.peto à te.

                                              Also

Also the Gerund in *do*, and the supine in *um*, is comprehended in this kind of speech. 2, *De Orat*. A dicendo refugisti. 1. *Epist*. Ab omnibus reclamatum est. Also in these two phrases following, it is spoken by the supine. Obsonatu redeo, cubitu resurgo. But this Oration is made much more elegant beeing spoken by the noune. *Caf*. A decimæ legionis cohortatione, à pabulationibus. Even as before it was more elegantly spoken, inter cœnam, and inter scyphos, then inter cœnandum, and inter potandum.

Cap. 16.

Of the rection of prepositions serving to both cases.

These prepositions following, do governe both an accusative and an Ablative case: but they doe governe an accusative case beeing ioyned with a verbe of motion, and an ablative case beeing ioyned with a Uerbe of quietnesse or rest.

In, with an accusative case. *In Brut*. In vitam paulò seriùs, tanquam in viam ingressus. 7. *Verr*. In carcerem includere. But this use is variable. 2. *Att*. Includere in carcere. 2. *Phil*. Incidere in æs. And 6. *Verr*. In ære. *Pro Planc*. Ponere in oppido. 3. *Phil*. ponere in possessionem. 7. *Att*. proponere in publico.

2. *Agra*. In publicum . In reos referre, as be-fore, Inter reos deferre. In annos singulos. 2 De *Orat*. In diem videre.

In, with an ablatiue case. 6. *Verr*. Non modò in ære alieno nullo, sed in suis nummis multis esse. With a Gerund in *do. Terent. And.* In denegando modò quis pudor est paululum? Notwithstanding some examples do admit an accusatiue case. *Terent. Adelph.* Vereor te in eos laudare. 1. *Ver*. hostilem in modum. 7. *V er* Præclara navis in speciem.

Sub, with an accusatiue case. 2. *Phil*. Sub scalas se conijcere. 3. *Fin*. Sub delectum cadere.

Sub, with an ablatiue case. *De Nat*. Homines sub terra habitantes, 10. *Epist*. Sub manu tabellarios habere.

Sometime also this preposition hath an accusatiue case with a verbe of quietnes, and an ablatiue with a verbe of motion. 3. *Ad Fratrem*. Est sub tectum. *De div*. Nullo posito simulacro sub oculis . This preposition sub, when it is ioyned to time , hath most commonly an accusatiue case. 2. *Fra*. Sub dies festos.   2. *Cæs*. 1 Sub vesperum.

Super and subter, 2. *Leg*. Super terræ tumulum. 1. *Tus*. Plato cupiditatem subter præcordia locavit. 16. *Att*. . Hac super re scribam ad te. 6. *Æneid*.

   --- *subter densa testudine*. ---

Procul, *Liv*. 13. *Lib*. Locus procul muros. 7. *Epist*.

Epist.Patria procul.*Colum*.Procul vero.

Clam.*Plau.in Ner*. Clam patrem, clam iis.
From whence commeth clanculum.

Verbes beeing compounded with Prepositions, doe often keepe the case of the preposition,
wherewith they be compounded. *Liv*. Te adeunt. *Cicero* doth most often repeat the preposition : as ingredi in vrbem. So *Terent*. Acce-
dere ad ignem.

Cap. 17.

Of the defect of prepositions.

THe defect of *Syntax* or construction, is understood before in divers partes. But the
defect of prepositions is almost usuall, in the
nounes of cause, and of measure, and in the proper names of Cities. Defect is more seldome
in the material cause.*Liv*.6.Capitolium quoque saxo quadrato substructum est. But defect is made frequent in the efficient cause. 2.
De Orat. Gloria clarus, authoritate gravis,
humanitate politus. 15. *Epist*. Suspensus ex-
pectatione.11.*Epist*.Captus dulcedine.3.*Leg*
Pendere spe cæca.(But also 8.*Att*.Pendere a-
nimi)9.*Att*.Angi expectatione. 12. *Phil*. Dis-
crutior amore.*Terent*. *Adelph*.Discrutior animi.

The ablative case of an instrument and of a
meane

meane is of this *sintax*, seeing that is a certaine
efficient. *Pro Mil.* Vulnus in latere quod acu
punctum videretur. *Pro Dom.* Lapidibus ap-
petere. 1. *Leg.* Cato ortu Tusculanus, civitate
Romanus. Wherunto doth pertaine ỹ gerund
in *do. Ter. Adel.* Defessus sum ambulando.

A speciall noune of measure is verye often
put in the accusative case, and sometime also in
the ablative *Cæs.7.* Fossas quinosdenos pedes
latas. *Plin.* Longum sesquipede, latum pede.
Idem. Mutis ducentos pedes altis, quinquagenos latis. *Cæs.7.* Turres quæ pedes octoginta inter se distarent. *Idem* 1. Millia passuum
tria ab eorum castris castra ponit, *Ibidem*, ho-
stes sub monte consedisse millia passuum ab
ipsius castris octo. In the which kind of speech
there is a defect of the Preposition per, secun-
dùm, oz in.

Notwithstanding a noune of excesse is onely
put in the ablative case. *Plaut. Trin.* Sesquipede est quàm tu longior.

The space of time, which is understood by
quamdiu, is put in the accusative case, as it
were a speciall noune of mesure. 2. *Phil.* Ab hinc
annos prope viginti. *Terent.* Ab hinc annos
quindecim : here ante doth seeme to be understood. And so in that speech, pridie compitalia,
postridie ludos. Grammarians do thinke that
ante and post is to be understood. And in these
the pzeposition is sometime expzessed. *Plin. lib.*

15. speaking of the apple which was brought from *Carthage* to *Rome*; Atqui tertium (sayth he)ante diem scitote decerptum Carthagine that is, ab hinc tertium diem. So these phrases of *Cicero*, aliquot jam per annos, per eos dies, per decem annos. *Liv.* Obsidio vix in paucos dies tollerabilis.

Sometime the ablative case is answered, but more seldome with *Cicero*. Pro Com. Roscium cum Fannio decidisse. Quo tempore? Ab hinc annis quindecim.

Notwithstanding a terme of time, which is understood by quando, is put onely in the ablative case. 2.*Verr.*Hora nona convenire cœpistis.*Pro Mil.* Clodius respondit triduo illum,ad summum quatriduo,periturum,*Tuscu.* Regnante Tarquinio superbo Pythagoras in Italiam venit. *Sal in 5.* Audito Marcium Regem proconsulem per Lycaoniam, cum tribus legionibus in Ciliciam tendere. *Virg.7.Æneid.*

- - - *Non vobis reges Latino*

Divitis uber agri Trojæque opulentia deerit. For all these thinges are expressed by quando:quando regnabat Tarquinius,quando auditum est,dum rex erit Latinus, *Mart.*

- - - *Et Bruto consule vina bibes.*

That is, vina nata dum Consul erat Brutus. And here also sometime the Preposition is added. *Terent. And.* Ferè in diebus paucis,quibus

bus hæc acta ſunt, *Idem.* Poſtremò & qua in
die parva perijſſet ſoror, 4. *Verr.* Non opinor,
id ages, vt iſta pecunia in quinquennio con-
ſumatur in ſtatuis. 2. *Frat.* Naviges de menſe
Decembri. *Pro Mur.* De noĉte vigilare. wherunto theſe **Phꝛaſes** following ſeeme to pertaine. *Terent. And.* In denegando modo quis
pudor eſt paululum? *Ibidem.* In cognoſcendo
tute ipſe aderis.

**And this is the abſolute rection of pꝛepoſiti-
ons of cauſe and meaſure: there remayneth
the like rection in pꝛoper names of Cowne,
which, foꝛ the variable differences of motion
and quietnes, are governed in a divers caſe.**

**The pꝛoper name of a Cowne, is put in the
accuſative caſe, if it do ſignifie moving oꝛ motion to a place: oꝛ in the ablative caſe, if ŷ motion be by a place oꝛ from a place.** 8. *Att.* Thea-
num, Sidicinum veniſſem. 3. *Tuſc.* Cumas ſe
contuliſſe dicitur, *Liv.* Carthaginem novam
in hyberna eſt deduĉtus . **Here the noune is
compounded.** *Idem lib.* 23. Capuam fleĉtit iter,
luxuriantem longa felicitate ac indulgentia
fortunæ. *Ad Att.* Iter Laodicia faciebam, 3.
Epiſt. Epiſtolas ad me Servilius Tarſo miſerat
**Sometime the Pꝛepoſition is added, that ther-
by the defect may be better knowne.** *Cæſ.* 1. Ad
Genevam pervenit. 6. *Verr.* Ad Meſſanam
tranſire, 2. *Acad.* Veniſſe à Roma. 4. *Ep.* Ab E-
pidauro navi adveĉtus , A Brunduſio uſque

que Romam.

If rest or quietnesse be signified, the proper name of a Towne, beeing either of the firste or second parisillable, declination and singular number, is put in the genitive case: but if it be either of the imparisyllable declinations, it shall be put in the dative or ablative case. Euery plurall shal be put in the ablative case. 3 E-pist.Cúm enim Laodiciæ,cum Apameæ, cum Synadis,cum philomeli,cum Iconij essem.17 Att.fuisse Carthagini.de So.Lacedæmone ho-nestissimũ esse præsidiũ senectutis.1.Off.Au-dientem Cratippum,idq; Athenis. Moreover to put it in the genitive or dative case, is accor-ding to vse,but not according to art. Notwith-standing in the ablative cases, a preposition may be understood: as in vulgar tongues, yea and in the Greek tongue also where the name of a towne is perpetually gouerned of a prepo-sition.But a preposition is added in the names of streetes.Cic.In Cumano cum essem.

Fewe nounes, not beeing proper names of Townes,doe follow the same syntax: as these accusative cases, domum,rus: ablative cases, domo,rure: genitive cases, domi,belli,mili-tiæ,humi, and both the dative and ablative case,ruri and rure.

With the genitive case domi, and the accu-satiue domum are ioyned, mea, tua, sua, no-stra,vestra,aliena,2.Phil.Pompejum domum suam

K

ſuam compuliſtis. 2. *De Orat.*Rus ex urbe e-
volare,*Teren,Eun.* Domo exulo. *In Piſo,* Me
domo mea expuliſtis. *Att.* Rure jam redie-
ram4,*Epiſt.*Nonne mavis ſine periculo domi
tuæ eſſe, quam cum periculo alienæ, 5. *Tuſc.*
Diodorus multos annos noſtræ domi vixit
3.*Verr.*Iactatur domi ſuæ vir optimus.7.*Att.*
Domi Cæſaris : and with ſuch like ſubſtan-
tibes.

Adiectibes are ſeldome conſtrued with thoſe
abſolute caſes, 16,*Att.*Malo cum timore domi eſſe,quàm ſine timore Athenis tuis.2,*Off.*
Quibuſcunque rebus vel domi vel belli po-
terunt,remp.augeant.5.*Tuſc.* Quorum virtus fuerat domi militiæq; cognita. 2.*Cat.*jacere humi.2.*Tuſc.*Nil mea intereſt, humi-ne
an ſublimé putreſcam,3 .*Off.* Ruri habitare.
13. Quam equidem rure eſſe arbitror. You
may find other nounes alſo in the ſame ſyntax.
Terent. Quæ quærere inſiſtam via ? *Pro Pom.*
Quantas ille res terra marique geſſerit.

CAP. 18.

Of proſodie and the true writing
of ſentences.

THe kindes of Syntax have beene hitherto
ſpoken of : there remayneth one difference
and diſtinction of true pronuntiation and wryting in a ſentence or oration, by clauſes and en-
terla-

terlaſing of pointes , which the ſhutting in of
the bꝛeath,and the ſtraightnes of the ſpirite,
haue cauſed.This inuention (ſaith *Tullie*)doth
fall out ſo ſweet,that although ſome man haue
an infinite ſpirite oꝛ bꝛeath , notwithſtanding
we will not haue him continue in ſpeaking,
without dꝛawing of the bꝛeath.

A diſtinction is of an imperfect oꝛ of a per⸗
fect ſentence. The diſtinction of an imperfect
ſentence,doth ſuſpend oꝛ ſtay the bꝛeath without bꝛeathing : and that is a ſubdiſtinction,
oꝛ a *Comma*. A ſubdiſtinction is that,where-
with is diſtinguiſhed by a litle oꝛ ſmal ſtaye oꝛ
pauſe of the bꝛeath,between the middle woꝛd,
which maye bee attributed doubtfullye to the
part going befoꝛe and comming after : and it
is noted with this little rodde oꝛ marke as
Summa quidem authoritate Philoſophi, ſe-
verè ſanè atque honeſté,hæc tria genera con-
fuſa cogitatione diſtingunt . A *Comma* oꝛ
ſhoꝛt member of a ſentence is that, whereby
anye ſentence going befoꝛe,is cut oꝛ ſevered
from the perfection of the ſentence following,
with a little longer pauſe , and is noted with
this halfe circle , as, Quicquid enim juſtum ſit , id etiam utile eſſe cenſent : itemque quod honeſtum , idem juſtum . The
Comma is often expꝛeſſed by a coniunction,
and therefoꝛe is not noted anye other wayes·
as,

*unà Euruſq̃, Notuſq̃, ruunt crebérq̃, procellis
Africus,& vaſtos tollunt ad littora fluctus.*

A *Parentheſis*,that is an interpoſition oꝛ ſhutting in,is alſo a ſhoꝛt member. *Pro Mil.* Vide
enim(nam tu aberas)noſtros cupere bellum
But it is noted on both ſides with halfe cir-
cles.The diſtinction of a perfect ſentence hath
a longer ſtaye of bꝛeathing,and ſurceaſeth the
bꝛeath: And it is a *colon* oꝛ a *period*. A *colon* oꝛ
member is that, whereby a perfect ſentence is
diſtinguiſhed, but being ioyned with an other,
with a leſſe time of the bꝛeath beeing ſtayed,
and it is to be noted with a point ſet at the top
of the letter,oꝛ els with two points. A *period*,
circle,circumſcription, oꝛ comprehenſion is, when
as the bꝛeath beeing wholly oꝛ altogeather
ſtayed and ended, the perfect ſentence is concluded: and the beginning thereof is noted
with a great letter, and the ende with a point
at the laſt letter thus put . As,Ammonius
regis legatus apertè pecunia nos oppugnat.
A *period* maye conſiſt of manye ſentences and
members, but that is longeſt, which can bee
pꝛonounced with one bꝛeath. But there is one
way of nature,an other of art: as it were a ful
compꝛehenſion of 4. examiters: foꝛ ſo it is de-
fined of *Tullie*.But let vs ioyne examples of all
diſtinctions,as

Summa quidem authoritate philoſophi ſe-
veré ſané atꝗ honeſté,hæc tria genera côfuſa
cogi-

cogitatione diſtinguunt: quicquid enim iuſtum ſit, id etiam utile eſſe cenſent: itemque quod honeſtum, idem juſtum: ex quo efficitur, ut quicquid honeſtum ſit, idem utile.

And alſo let this be an example of all interlaced pointes.

Arma virumq̃, cano, Trojæ qui primus ab oris
Italiam fato profugus Laviniaq̃, venit
Litora.multum ille & terris jactatus & alto,
Vi ſuperúm, ſævæ memorem Iunonis ob iram,
Multa quoq̃, & bello paſſus, dum cōderent urbē,
Inſerretq̃, deos Latio, genus unde Latinum,
Albanique patres atq̃, altæ mœnia Romæ.

This periode is ſomewhat long: yet ſo, that it may be pronounced with one breath continued. Therefore the voyce is diligently to be exerciſed from young yeares or childhode, that it may ſuffice for any great periodes. And the example of *Demoſthenes* is eſpecially to be looked upon and to be imitated: in whom, as it is ſayd in *Oratorio ſecundo*, there was ſo great ſtudie and ſo great labour, that he could overcome the wantes or impedimentes of nature by induſtrie and diligence: and when as he was ſuch a ſtutterer, that he could not ſpeake the firſt letter of the Art which he ſtudied, he brought to paſſe by meditating, that no man was thought to ſpeake more playnely then he.

Afteꝛ

Afterward when his breath was straighter,
he obteined so much in conteinyng his breath,
that in one continuaunce of wordes (as his
writynges declare) he conteineth two con-
tentions and remissions of his voyce . Moreover (as it is left in writyng) litle stones beyng cast into his mouth, he was wont to pronounce with a great voyce many verses,
with one breath : neither staying in
a place , but walkyng up and
downe , yea and that
goyng by a steepe
ascent or very
hygh.

The end of P. Ramus
Grammar.

THE RVDIMENTES

OF P. RAMVS

his Latine GRAMMAR.

ENGLISHED AND
newly corrected,

Seene and alowed.

GODISMY DEFENDER.

AT LONDON.

Printed by Robert Walde-graue.

1585.

¶ RVDIMENTES
OF THE LATINE
Grammar, written by
P. R a m v s,

Discipulus.

Pray you Maister (if it be not troublesome to you) teache me those things shortly, which others set down more at large, concerning Grammar?

Magister.

Nothing truely, can be more pleasaunt to me, than to fulfill this thy so liberall and honest request.

D Shal I then aske you of everye thing simplye?

M This pleaseth me very well: For so I shal both know thy wit, and thou shalt perceive my studie.

D What is Grammar?

M It is an art to speake well.

D Howe manye partes are there of Grammar?

2   M Two,

M Two, *Etymology* and *Sintax.*

D What is *Etymology?*

M It is the first parte of Grammar, which doeth interpreat the properties of wordes set alone one by one, without anye other ioyned thereto.

D what is a worde?

M It is a note by which everye thing is called.

D whereof is a worde made?

M Of a sillable.

D what is a syllable?

M It is a full or perfecte sound in a word, as for example, Dos, flos : so likewise, in Dominus there are three syllables, do—mi—nus

D whereof is a syllable made?

M Of a letter.

D what is a letter?

M It is a sounde which in a syllable cannot be devided.

D Howe manye kindes of letters are there?

M Two: bowels and consonants,

D what is a vowel:

M It is a letter which may make a syllable by himselfe, as *a. e. i.* pronounced with open mouth, and also *o. v. y.* pronounced with the mouth drawen together.

D What is a Consonant?

M It is a letter which can make a syllable, onely when it hath a vowell ioyned with him,

as

as *b. c. d.*

D How many kinds of Consonants are there?

M Two: Semi-vowels and Mutes.

D What is a Semi-vowell?

M It is a Consonant which maketh a sound, halfe like the sound of a vowell.

D How manye kindes of semi-vowelles are there?

M Two: liquides, and firme semi-vowels.

D What is a *Liquid*?

M It is a semi-vowell, which is pronounced with the lips opened, somewhat like the first sort of vowels, and his sound sometime is more flat, and as it were melteth, whereupon it is called liquide, as *l. m. n. r. s.*

D Howe manye kindes of liquides are there?

M Two: some are sharpe liquides as *r. s. l,* this hissing in certaine Greek words is writtē double by this Greeke character, *z,* as in zopirus and zephirus, some are more flatt liquides as *m* and *n.*

D What is a firme semi-vowell?

M It is a semi-vowell which is pronounced with the lippes drawne together somewhat like the second sort of vowelles, and it hath an vnchaungeable sound for which cause it is called firme as *ef* and *jod, vau.*

D What is a *mute?*

M It is a consonant which onely muttereth a certaine indevour to speake.

3   D How

D How many kinds of *mutes* are there?

M Two: opened *mutes*, and shut *mutes*.

D What is an open *mute*?

M It is a *mute* which muttereth more softly, the lippes beeing opened, partly in the teeth, as *t*, and *d*, partlye in the roofe of the mouth, as *c*, *q*, *g*: *k*, which is not used in Latine wordes, and *q*, in sound are altogether the same with *c*: here in like maner there is one figure in writing cal=led *x*, put for the two consonauntes *cs*, or *gs*, as in crux and frux which is knowne by their cases crucis and frugis.

D What is a shut *mute*?

M It is a *mute* which muttereth within the cheeke, the lippes beeing close shut togeather, as *b*, and *p*: *h*, is a marke of breathing. And thus the letters are devided, which are thus numbred, *a*, *b*, *c*, *d*, *e*, *f*, *g*, *h*, *i*, *k*, *l*, *m*, *n*, *o*, *p*, *q*, *r*, *s*, *t*, *u*, *x*, *y*, *z*, vnto which adde *jod* and *uav*, beeing con=sonautes and they are in number twentye and fiue.

Cap. 2.

Of the making and quantity of sylla-bles.

D BEcause you haue declared the Letters teach me now how many kinds of *sylla-bles* there are?

M Three: of one vowel qnly, as, *a*, *e*, *i*, *o*, *u*, *y*, or of two,

two, and therefore it is called a *Dipthong* as *a.œ. au. eu.* in ætas, æstrum, audio, euge, or compounded of a vowell, and a Consonant, sometime of two, as As, sometimes of three, as Ars, sometimes of foure, as mars, sometimes of siue. as stans, sometimes of sixe, as Stirps.

D Now I knowe the making of a *sillable*, teach me the quantitie?

M Every *sillable* is either shorte or long: a shorte *sillable* is that which consisteth of one time, as the first *sillable* in this noune Deus, and it hath this marke ouer the vowell if neede require, ˘

D What is a long *sillable*?

M It is a syllable which standeth of two times, as the first *sillable* in audi, and in veruex: and if neede require, hath this marke ouer it ‐

Cap. 3.

Of Accent and Notation.

D *I* Understande the partes of a worde, which are the common affections of a worde?

M *Accent* and *Notation*.

D What is *Accent*?

M It is a common affection of a word, whereby the word is as it were tuned, and there is but one *Accent* in one syllable of euerye worde, although the worde be made of divers syllables.

D Howe manye kindes of *Accents* are there?

4   M Three

M Thꝛee: one ſharpe, by which a ſyllable is lift up, another heavie, by which a ſillable is depꝛeſſed, the thiꝛd a circumflect, by which a ſillable is both lift vp and alſo depꝛeſſed, and if need require, every one of them is thus marked, a ſharpe *Accent* thus a heavie *Accent* thus a *Circumflect* thus ^

D What is *Notation*?

M It is a common affection of a woꝛde, by which the kinde oꝛ figure of a woꝛde is ſought out.

D What is the kinde?

M It is that, by which wee ſeeke out whether a woꝛde be a *Primitiue*, as Amo, oꝛ a *Deriuatiue*, deriued of ſome *Primitiue*, as Amabilis.

D What is the figure?

M It is that by which it is ſought, whether the woꝛd be a ſimple oꝛ a compounde woꝛde, a ſimple, as Amo, doctus, a compound, as Redamo, perdoctus.

Cap. 4.

Of a Novne and his Genders.

D I haue heard what a woꝛd is, which bee the partes of a woꝛd in ſyllables : which bee the leſſe partes in Letters : which be the pꝛoper accidentes in notation: Nowe ſhewe me the kindes of woꝛdes.

M Euery

M Every word is eyther a word hauing number or without number.

D What is a worde hauing number?

M It is a word which ouer and besides his proper English, signifieth a number eyther singular or plurall, whereupon it is called a worde of the singular or plural number.

D What is the singuler number.

M It is a number by which one thing alone, may be expressed: as Doctus, Legit.

D what is the plurall number?

M It is the number by which many thinges may be expressed: as docti, legunt.

D How manye kindes of wordes are there which haue number.

M Two, a Nowne and a verbe.

D What is a nowne?

M It is a word of number which hath gender and case.

D what is a Gender:

M It is the difference of a Nowne accoding to the sex, and it is simple or manifolde: that which is simple, is naturall or seyned: a naturall Gender is eyther masculine or feminine.

D what is a nowne of the masculine gender.

M It is a Nowne before which hic may bee set, as hic magister.

D what is a Nowne of the feminine Gender?

M Before which hæc may be set, as hæc musa:but som-times the masculine, som-times the feminine Gender are doubtfully used, and the same gender agreeth to either kinde, as aquila signifyng the hee Eagle, or the shee eagle is the feminine gender: passer a Cocke Sparrow, or a henne Sparrow is the masculine. For discerning of which kindes we adde the wordes mas or femina.

D what is a noune of the feigned or neuter gender?

M It is a Noune before which hoc maye be, set, as hoc templum.

D How is the manifolde gender devided?

M Into the common of the two first genders, and the common of all three.

D what is a noune of the common of two genders?

M It is a Noune, before which, hic & hæc may be set, as hic & hæc ciuis.

D What is a Noune of the Common of three Genders?

M It is a Noune before which hic hæc & hoc may be set, as hic hæc & hoc fœlix,

D How is a Noune devided by the difference of the Gender?

M Into a *Substantive* or an *Adjective*.

D What is a Noune *Substantive*?

M It is a Noune of one Gender or of two at the most, as hic pater : hic & hæc civis.

D What is an *Adjective*?

M It

M It is a Noune declined with three Genders, either in one ending: as hic hæc & hoc Fœlix, oʒ in two endinges, as hic & hæc fortis,& hoc forte, oʒ in three endings, as bonus bona,bonum.

Cap. 5.

Of the Comparison of Adject.

D *W*hat belongeth to manye of the *Adjectives?*

M *Comparisone.*

D How manye degrees of *comparisone* are there?

M After the absolute,there are two degrees named,the *comparative,* and the *superlative.*

D What is the *comparative* degree?

M It is a degree of *comparison* which is declared by the absolute degree,having magis ioyned therwith,as doctior,magis doctus.

D What is the *superlative* degree?

M It is a degree which is declared by the absolute degree having maxime joyned therewith, as doctissimus, maxime doctus, either degree is formed of the end of the absolute in *i:* the comparative by putting to *or,* foʒ the common gender,ant *us,* foʒ the neuter, as of docti, doctior,doctius. The superlative is formed by putting to *ssimus* foʒ the masculine, *ssima,*foʒ the feminine,*ssimum* foʒ the neuter, as doctissimus,

doctis-

doctissima, doctissimum, fortissimus, fortissima, fortissimum: but if the absolute end in *er*, the superlatiue masculine is made by putting to *rimus*, the feminine *rima*, the neuter *rimum*, as niger, nigerrimus, nigerrima, nigerrimum.

If a vowell come before *us*, it is compared onely by magis and maxime, as pius, magis pius, maxime pius.

Cap. 6.

Of Diminution.

D *What* belongeth to certaine substantiues?
M Diminution.

D What is a noune diminutiue.

M It is a noune which without comparison signifieth in the same kind a diminishing of his primitiue, and it endeth either in *io*, as of homo homuncio, or in *us*, as of filio, filiolus, beeing masculines, or in *a*, as anima, animula, being feminines, or in *um* as caput capitulum, beeing neuters, or in *ter*, as surdaster, Antoniaster, parasitaster, which are more seldome in vse.

Cap. 7.

Of Case and the first Declension beeing of euen sillables.

D I Haue heard the Genders, and of comparisons, and Diminution by the Genders

ders

vers: what is a case?

M It is a speciall ending of a Nowne.

D How many cases are there?

M Sixe in both numbers the Nominatiue, the Genitiue, the Datiue, the Accusatiue, the Vocatiue & the Ablatiue: the Nominatiue and the Vocatiue are much like in both numbers, the Datiue and the Ablatiue are like in the plurall number, as magister magister, magistri magistri, magistris, magistris. In Nownes of the neuter gender these three, the Nominatiue, the Accusatiue, and the Vocatiue, are like in both numbers, and in the plurall number they ende all in *a*, as templum templa, tempus tempora.

D The declining of a Nowne by the cases how is it called?

M A Declension.

D How many kinds of Declensions are there?

M Two: one hauing euen sillables, an other hauing vn-euen sillables.

D VVhat is a Declension hauing euen sillables?

M It is a declension whose Datiue case plurall ending in *is*, hath euen sillables with the Nominatiue singular, as musa musis, dominus dominis.

D How many kindes of declensions are there which haue euen sillables?

M Two: the first which hath the nominatiue singular

singular ending in *a*, of the feminine gender for
the most part, the genitive in *e*, the dative in *e*,
the accusative in *am*, the ablative in *a*, the nominative plurall in *e*, the genitive in *arum*, the
Accusative in *as*, as musa, musæ, musæ, musam,
musa, musa.   Musæ, musarum, musis, musas, musæ musis.

CAP. 8.

Of the second Declension of even silla-
bles.

D *W*hat is the second Declension of even
sillables?

M It is a Declension which in the nominative case singular endeth in *s*, or *r*, of the masculine gender for the most part, or *m*, of the neuter, ẏ genitive in *i*, the Dative in *o*, the Accusative in *um*, the Nominative plural in *i*, the genitive in *orum*, the accusative in *os*.

D Give me an exãple of the Nominative case
ending in *s*?

M Dominus, domini, domino, dominũ, domine, domino : Domini, dominorum, dominis, dominos, domini, dominis, *us* in the Uocatiue case is chaunged into *e*, these three ends
in *i*, filius, fili, genius, geni, meus, mi, deus is
not chaunged in the Uocatiue. *us* is taken away
from proper nounes in *s*, as Antonius, Antoni.

D Give me an exãple of the Nominative case
ending

ending in r?

M Nounes end in r, three maner of waies, in *er* *ir*, *ur*: in *er*, as magister, magistri, magistro, magistrū, magister, magistro: Magistri, magistrorum, magistris, magistros, magistri, magistris. In *ir*, there is one onely ending as , vir, viri, viro virum, vir, viro: Viri, virorum, viris, viros, viri, viris. In like maner in *ur*, there is one onely ending, as satur, saturi, saturo, saturum, satur, saturo: Saturi, saturorum, saturis, saturos, saturi, saturis.

D Give me an example of the Nominative case ending in *m*?

M Scamnum, scamni, scamno, scamnum, scamnum, scamno: scamna, scamnorum, scamnis, scamna, scamnis.

Cap. 9.

Of Adjectives of even sillables which follow not the right rule.

D I Have plainely vnderstood those thinges which you haue spoken of the first Declension hauing even *sillables*, of what Declension are *Adjectiues* of even *sillables*?

M Of both the Declensions which have even *sillables*, but of divers Genders , as bonus, bona , bonum, and of them twentye and one commonlye called Pronounes follow not the right rule, but especially these three, ego, tu sui.

Ego,

{ Ego,mei oʒ mis, mihi oʒ mi,me,me,
{ Nos,noſtrum oʒ noſtri,nobis, nos nobis.
{ Tu,tui oʒ tis,tibi,te,tu,te
{ Vos,veſtrum oʒ veſtri,vobis,vos,vobis.
{ Sui,ſibi,ſe,ſe
{ Sui,ſibi,ſe,ſe.

This third woʒde wanteth the Nominatiue
and vocatiue caſe of both numbers:of theſe thʒee
do ariſe fiue,which follow the right rule, meus,
mea,meum,noſter,noſtra,noſtrum, tuus,tua,
tuum,veſter, veſtra, veſtrum, ſuus, ſua, ſuum.
Theſe folowing haue ther genitiues in *us*,their
Datiues in *i*,the thʒee firſt haue their genitiues
in *ius*.

{ Hic,hæc,hoc.   { Hi,hæ,hæc,
{ Huius,   { Horum,harū,horum,
{ Huic,   { His,
{ Hunc,hanc,hoc,   { Hos,has,hæc,
{ Hoc,hac,hoc,   { His.

{ Is,ea,id,   { Ei,oʒ ij,ſomtimes i,eæ,ea
{ Eius,   { Eorum,earum, eorum,
{ Ei,   { Eis,oʒ ijs,ſometimes is,
{ Eum,eam,id,   { Eos,eas,ea,
{ Eo,ea,eo,   { Eis oʒ ijs,ſometimes is.

In like maner idem , eadem, idem, a compound hereof is declined.

{ Quis oʒ qui,quæ oʒ   { Quem,quam,quod
{   qua,quod oʒ quid   {   oʒ quid,
{ Cuius,   { Quo, qua , quo, ſome-
{ Cui,   { times alſo qui in every
                         Gender.   Qui

{ Qui,quæ,quæ oʒ qua,   { Quos, quas, quæ
  Quorum,quarum,   oʒ qua,
   quorum,   Quibus oʒ quæis.
{ Quibus oʒ queis,

The Adiectiues following ende in *ius* in the genitiue case, Iste,ista,istud: istius: isti. Ille,illa, illud: illius: illi: Ipse,ipsa,ipsum: ipsius: ipsi, Ali-us,alia, aliud: alius: alij, alter,altera,alterum: alterius: alteri. unus,una, unum: unius: uni: and ȳ Deriuatiues hereof ullus ulla, ullum: nullus, nulla, nullum, uter, utra, utrum, ȳ the cōpounds hereof, uterque, utraq;, utrunque: neuter, neu-tra, neutrum: solus, sola, solum: totus, tota, to-tum. Eight of these, Alius, alter, hic, is, iste, ille, ipse, qui, are Relatiues of some thinges going befoʒe: also thʒee are Demonstratiues Hic, ille, ipse: but sui and suus haue respect backe to the thing going befoʒe, as Omnis natura est con-servatrix sui.

Ambo and Duo are thus declined.

{ Ambo,ambæ,ambo,
  Amborum,ambarum,amborum,
  Ambobus,ambabus,ambobus,
  Ambos,ambas,ambo,
  Ambo,ambæ,ambo,
{ Ambobus,ambabus,ambobus.
{ Duo,duæ,duo,
  Duorum,duarum,duorum,
{ Duobus,duabus,duobus,

           B   Duos

{ Duos,duas,duo,
{ Duo,duæ,duo,
{ Duobus,duabus,duobus.

Cap. 10.

Of the Declensions having un-even sil-
    lables.

D ¶ Perceive your teaching concerning the
        Declensions of even sillables : now shew
me the Declensions of un-even sillables?

M The Declensions of un-even sillables are
those whose Dative cases plurall have un-even
sillables, with the Nominative case singular, &
the Genitive case singular endeth in *is*, the Dative in *i*, the Accusative in *em*, the Ablative in
e, or *i*, the Nominative and the Accusative plurall in *es*, the Genitive in *um*, or *ium*, the Dative and the Ablative in *ibus*.

D How many Declensions of un-even sillables are there?

M Two : the first whose Genitive case singular doth not encrease, and the wordes doe ende
in *e*, in the Nominative case singular, as Mantile, mantilis, or in *es*, as vulpes, vulpis, or in *is*,
as corbis, corbis, or in *er*, as Venter, ventris,
ventri, ventrem, venter, ventre : ventres, ven-
trum, ventribus, ventres, ventres, ventribus.

D what is the second Declension of un-even
sillables?

                                        M The

M The second is, whose genetive case singular doth encrease either by *a*, as Civitas, civitatis,,civitati,civitatem,civitas, civitate: civitates,civitatum and civitatium, civitatibus, civitates, civitates,civitatibus: or by *e*, as res,rei: or by *i*, as cinis cineris, or by *o*, as labor laboris, or by *v*, as virtus,virtutis, or by *y*, as calyx,calycis.

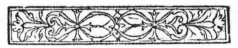

The ſeconde Booke of P.
RAMVS HIS
Rudimentes.

Cap. I.
Of a Verbe.

D Me thinketh I know a certaine *Etymology* of Nouncs, I doe earnestlye desire to know the like doctrine of *verbes*, tel me therefore what is a *verbe*?

M It is a word of number; with *tenſe* and *perſon*.

D what is *Tenſe*?

M It is ÿ difference of a *verbe*, according to the time Present, the time past, and the time to come. Everie present-tenſe is passing, but

not paſt: the Pꝛeter-tenſe and the future-tenſe
are partly not paſt, and partly fully paſt. Therefoꝛe of this *verbe* finite, there are thꝛee tenſes
not paſt, and as many fully paſt, and every one
of them al-moſt are double. *The tenſes not paſt,*
as the firſt pꝛeſent-tenſe, amo, amor: the ſecond,
amem, amer: the firſt Pꝛeter-tenſe, amabam, a-
mabar: the ſecond amarem, amarer: of the firſte
Pꝛeter-tenſe not paſte, doth ariſe a Noune participle, *bam* oꝛ *bar*, beeing chaunged into *ns*: as of
amabam, ſedebam, loquebar, cōmeth amans,
ſedens, loquens. The firſt future, amabo, amabor: the ſecond, ama, amare, amato, amator.
Yet amem, and amer, maye alſo be of the Future-tenſe, as well as amarem, and amarer.
The ſecond and the third perſon ſingular of the
ſecond Future is all one, as amato, amator.

The tenſes fully paſt: as the firſt Pꝛeter-tenſe,
amavi: the ſecond amaverim: the third amaveram: the fourth amaviſſem: the future amaverim oꝛ amavero: and in the other perſons, as in
the ſecond pꝛeter-perfectenſe. Foꝛ this is alſo
ambiguous, as amem and amarem.

D whereof is the firſt time perfectly paſt foꝛ-
med?

M Of the ſecond parſon of the Pꝛeſent-time,
ẙ laſt letter *s*, being chaunged into *vi*, as amas,
amavi, fles, flevi, petis, petivi, audis, audivi.

D How many kindes of *Anomalies* are there
of

of the Preterperfect-tense.

M These two are most common the first when *u*, is turned into *u*, the vowel going before beeing taken awaye, as domas, domui for domavi, so habes, habui, alis, alui, salis, salui. The second when as *u*, is taken awaye with the vowell going before, as juvas, juvi, moves, movi, defendis, defendi, comperis, comperi.

D How many kindes of *Infinitive* verbes are there?

M Two: one *perpetuall* and an other *participiall*. *Perpetuall* which is varied by re, or ri, in the present time, as amare, amari, by *se* in the time past, as amavisse. *Participiall*, which is declined like a case of a Noune, and it is either a Gerund or a Supine.

D What is a Gerund.

M Which in the Present-tense and Pretertense is declined in *di*, or *do*, and in the Future-tense in *dum*. The first is formed of the first finitive time past not finished, *bam* or *bar*, beeing chaunged into *ndi*, as amabam, amandi, sedebam, sedendi, loquebar, loquendi, of the firste Gerund ending in *di*, the two other Gerundes come, which ende in *do* or *dum*. Of a Gerunde commeth a Gerundine noune in *dus*, *da*, *dum*, as tuendus, tuenda, tuendum.

D What is a Supine?

M which is varied in *u*, the present-tense & the preter-tense, & in *um*, in the future-tense, as amatu, amatum.

D Whereof is the first Supine formed?

M Of the first finitive preterperfec-tense, the last sillable *vi*, being changed into *tu*, as amavi, amatu, juvi, jutu, flevi, fletu, movi, motu, petivi, petitu, audivi, auditu. The two last vowels *u i*, are chaunged into *itu*, as domui, domitu, habui, habitu, alui, alitu, salui salitu or saltu.

The supines of deponents are formed of feigned preter-tenses, as insidiatu, fruitu, veritu, mentitu, are formed as if there were read insidiavi, verui, fruivi, mentivi. Hereof doth proceede a Noune, by putting to *s* of the Passive or Deponent signification, Amatus, loquutus.

D Whereof is the second Supine formed?

M Of the first, by putting to *m*, as of amatu, amatum. Hereof springeth the noune in *rus*, by changing *m*, into *rus*, as of amatum, amaturus.

D What is a person?

M It is a speciall end of a Verbe.

D How many persones are there?

M Three in both numbers, the firste singular amo, the second amas, the third amat: the firste plurall amamus, the second amatis, the thirde amant, whereof a verbe is called personall: but impersonalls have the third person singular only, as pœnitet, amarur, which follow the lawe of their originall theames.

D How manye kindes of verbes Personalls are there?

M Two

M Two.

D Which is the first kinde?

M when the verbe endeth in *o*, and if *o*, maye be changed into *or*, it is an active, as amo, amor if it cannot, it is called a Neuter, as sedeo.

D which is the second forme or kind?

M The second is, when the verb endeth in *or*, and if it may be chaunged into *o*, it is a Passive, as amo, amor, otherwise it is called a Deponent, as loquor.

Passives and *Deponents* want Pretertenses.

Cap. 2.

Of the first Conjugation in bo.

D The declining of a verbe according to Tenses, and persons how is it called?

M A Conjugation.

D Howe many kindes of Conjugations are there?

M Two: one in *bo*, another in *am*.

D what is a Conjugation in *bo*.

M whose first Future-tense not past, doth end in *bo* or *bor*: and it is formed of the second person singular of the first present-tense, by turning *ſ* or *ris* into *bo* or *bor*, as amas, amaris: amabo, Amabor, Fles, Fleris; Flebo, Flebor.

D How many Conjugations are there in *bo*?

M Two: the first whose second person singular, of the first present-tense doth end in *as*, being

4   an

an Active o2 in *aris* being a Passive.

D ❦Give an example of the first fo2me?

M Amo, I love, amas, amat : amamus amatis, amant.

Amem, I may loue, ames, amet : amemus a metis, ament.

Amarem, I might o2 coulde love, amares, a maret: amaremus, amaretis, amarent

Amabam, I did love, amabas, amabat: amabamus, amabatis, amabant.

Amabo, I shall o2 will love, amabis, amabit amabimus, amabitis, amabunt.

Ama o2 amato, Love thou, amato: amate o2 amatote, amanto.

Amavi, I have loved, amavisti amavit : amavimus, amavistis, amaverunt o2 amavere.

Amaverim, I might o2 should have loved, amaveris, amaverit: amaverimus, amaveritis, amaverint.

Amaveram, I had loved, amaveras, amaverat: amaveramus, amaveratis, amaverant.

Amavissem, I might o2 should have had loved, amavisses, amavisset: amavissemus, amavissetis, amavissent.

Amavero, I may o2 can love hereafter, amaveris, amaverit: amaverimus, amaveritis, amaverint.

Amare to love, amavisse to have o2 had loved:
Amandi, of loving, amando, in loving, amandum, to be loved.

Ama-

Amatu, to be beloued amatum, to loue.

D Giue an example of the second forme?

M Amor, I am loued, amaris or amare, a-
matur: amamur, amamini, amantur.

Amer, I may or can be loued, ameris or amere, ametur: amemur, amemini, amentur,

Amarer, I should or wold be loued, amareris,
or amarere, amaretur: amaremur, amaremini
amarentur.

Amabar, I was loued, amabaris or amabare, amabatur: amabamur, amabamini, amabantur.

Amabor, I shall or will be loued, amaberis
or amabere, amabitur: amabimur, amabimini
amabuntur.

Amare, or amator, be thou loued, amator: a-
mamini, amantor.

CAP. 3.

Of the second Conjugation
in Bo.

D What is the second Conjugation?
M whose second person singuler of the
first present time endeth in *es*, or *eris* with ē
long.

D Giue an example of the first forme.

M Fleo, I weep, fles, flet: Flemus, fletis, flent,

Fleam, I may or can weepe, fleas, fleat: fleamus, fleatis, fleant.

Fle-

Flebam, I wept oz did weepe, flebas, flebat: flebamus, flebatis, flebant.

Flerem, I might oz should weepe, fleres, fleret: fleremus, fleretis, flerent.

Flebo, I shal oz will weep, flebis, flebit: flebimus, flebitis, flebunt.

Fle oz fleto, weep thou, fleto: flete oz fletote, flento.

Flevi, I have wept, flevisti, flevit : flevimus, flevistis, fleverunt oz flevere.

Fleverim, I might oz could have wept, fleveris, fleverit: fleverimus fleveritis, fleverint.

Fleveram, I had wept, fleveras, fleverat : fleveramus, fleveratis, fleverant.

Flevissem, I might oz should have had wept, flevisses, flevisset: flevissemus, flevissetis, flevissent.

Flevero, I may oz shall weepe hereafter, fleveris, fleverit : fleverimus, fleveritis, fleverint.

Flere, to weep, flevisse, to have oz had wept.

Flendi, of weeping, flendo, flendum.

Fletu, fletum.

D Giue an example of the secoud fozme?

M Fleor, I am be-wayled, fleris oz flert, fletur: flemur, flemini, flentur.

Flear, I may oz can be-wayled, flearis oz fleare, fleatur: fleamur, fleamini, fleantur.

Flebar, I was be-wailed, flebaris oz flebare flebatur: flebamur, flebamini, flebantur.

Flerer, I should oz would be be-wailed, flereris

ris oʒ flerere, fleretur: fleremur, fleremini, fle-
rentur.

Flebor, I shall oʒ will be be-wayled, fleberis
oʒ flebere, flebitur: flebimur, flebimini, fle-
buntur.

Flere oʒ fletor, be thou be-wayled, fletor: flemini, flentor.

Fleri, to be be-wayled.

Cap. 4.

Of the first Coniugation in *am*.

D *W*hat is a Coniugation in *am*?

M whose first Future-tense not past en-
deth in *am* oʒ in *ar*, and it is formed of the firste
person singular of the first present-tense, This
vowell *o*, oʒ this sillable *or*, beeing chaunged into *am* oʒ *ar*, as Peto, petam, audio, audiam: petor, petar, audior, audiar.

D How many Coniugations are there in *am*?

M Two: the firste whose second person singular of the first present-tense, doth end in *is* oʒ in
eris short: as petis, peteris.

D Give an example of the first forme.

M Peto, I desire, petis, petit : petimus, petitis, petunt.

Petam, I may oʒ can desire, petas, petat : petamus, petatis, petant.

Petebam, I did desire, petebas, petebat: petebamus, petebatis, petebant.

Pete-

Peterem, I might or ſhould deſire, peteres, peteret:peteremus,peteretis,peterent.

Petam,I ſhall or will deſire,petes,petet:petemus,petetis,petent.

Pete or petito deſire thou, petito ꞏ petite or petitote,petunto.

Petivi,I haue deſired,petiviſti,petivit : petivimus,petiviſtis, petiverunt or petiuere.

Petiverim,I might or ſhould have deſired,petiveris,petiverit: petiverimus,petiveritis,petiverint.

Petiveram,I had deſired,petiveras,petiverat: petiveramus,petiveratis,petiverant.

Petiviſſem, I might or ſhoulde have had deſired,petiviſſes,petiviſſet: petiviſſemus,petiviſſetis,petiviſſent.

Petivero,I ſhall or will deſire, petiveris, petiverit:petiverimus,petiveritis,petiverint.

Petere,to deſire:Petiviſſe,to have or had deſired

Petendi,of deſiring,petendo,petendum.

Petitu,to be deſired,petitum.

D Giue an example of the ſecond forme?

M Petor,I am deſired,peteris or petere,petitur:petimur,petimini,petuntur.

Petar,I may or can be deſired, petaris or petare,petatur:petamur,petamini,petantur.

Petebar,I was deſired,petebaris,or petebare,petebatur : petebamur, petebamini,petebantur.

Peterer,I ſhould or would be deſired, petere-
ris

ris oꝛ peterere, peteretur: peteremur, petere-
mini. peterentur.

Petar, I ſhall oꝛ will be deſired, peteris oꝛ petere, petetur: petemur, petemini, petentur.

Peti foꝛ Peteri, which *Analogy* is obſerued in
the reſt of this Conjugation.

CAP. 5.

Of the irregularity of Edo, Sum, Vo-
lo, Fero.

D HOw many *Anomalies* cheefely are there
of this Conjugation?

M Fowꝛe, Edo, Sum, Volo, Fero.

D How is Edo Conjugated.

M Edo I eate, es eſt: edimus, editis, edunt.
In like manner, Edam, ederem edebam, oꝛ
eſſem.

Es oꝛ ede, eate thou, edite or eſte.

Edi, ederim, ederam: ediſſem, edero, eſſe,
ediſſe

Edendi, Edendo, edendum: Eſu eſum oꝛ eſtu
eſtum, and Comedo (in like manner: as Seruius ſayth) and alſo the Paſſive foꝛme is fullye
declined.

D Conjugat Sum?

M Sum I am, es, eſt: ſumus, eſtis, ſunt.
Sim I may oꝛ can be, ſis, ſit: ſimus, ſitis,
ſint.

Eram

Eram I was, eras, erat: eramus, eratis, erant, wherof ens a Participle commeth, but the compounds thereof are most usuall.

Essem, I might or could be, esses, esset: essemus, essetis, essent. For the same, we say Forem, fores, foret, forent.

Ero, I shall or will be, eris, erit: erimus, eritis, erunt.

Es or esto be thou, esto: este or estote sunto, Site, is used for este of some old writers.

Fui I have beene, fuisti, fuit: fuimus, fuistis, fuerunt or fuere, of the old verbe fuo.

Fuerim, I should or would haue been, fueris, fuerit: fuerimus, fueritis, fuerint.

Fueram I had beene, fueras, fuerat: fueramus, fueratis, fuerant

Fuissem, I should or would haue had bene, fuisses, fuisset: fuissemus, fuissetis, fuissent.

Fuero, I shall or will bee heereafter, fueris, fuerit: fuerimus, fueritis, fuerint,

Esse, to be, fuisse, to haue or had beene, and of forem: fore.

In like maner affore, confore, Defore, Profore, whereof is the Future-tense.

D Conjugate Volo.

M Volo, I will, vis, vult: volumus, vultis, volunt. The Contractes heereof, Sis, captis, sultis for si vis, cape si vis, si vultis.

Velim, I may or can will, Velis, velit: velimus, velitis, velint,

                                            Vole-

Volebam, I did will, volebas volebat: Volebamus, volebatis, volebant.

Vellem, I might or shoulde will, velles, vellet:vellemus, velletis, vellent.

Volam, I shall will, voles, volet: volemus, voletis, volent.

Volui, I have willed, voluisti, voluit : voluimus, voluistis, voluerunt or voluere.

Voluerim, I woulde or shoulde have willed, volueris, voluerit:voluerimus, volueritis, voluerint.

Volueram, I had willed, volueras, voluerat: volueramus, volueratis, voluerant.

Voluissem, I might or shoulde haue had wil, voluisses, voluisset:voluissemus, voluissetis, voluissent.

Voluero, I shall will heereafter, volueris, voluerit : voluerimus, volueritis, voluerint.

Velle, to will, voluisse, to haue willed.

D Giue me those that followe the *Analogy* of this Uerbe.

M Malo, Nolo.

D Conjugat Malo.

M Malo, I do rather, mavis, mavult:malumus, mavultis, malunt.

Malim, I may or can rather, malis, malit: malimus, malitis, malint.

Malebam, I did rather, malebas, malebat: malebamus, malebatis, malebant.

Mallem,

Mallem, J might oȝ shoulde rather, malles, mallet:mallemus,malletis,mallent.

Malam,J will rather, males, malet: malemus,maletis,malent.

Malui, J haue rather,maluisti, maluit: maluimus,maluistis,maluerunt oȝ maluere.

Maluerim,J might oȝ shoulde haue rather, malueris, maluerit: maluerimus, malueritis, maluerint.

Malueram,J had rather, malueras, maluerat:malueramus,malueratis,maluerant.

Maluissem,J might oȝ shoulde haue had rather,maluisses,maluisset:maluissemus, maluissetis,maluissent.

Maluero, J shall oȝ will rather, malueris, maluerit:maluerimus,malueritis,maluerint.

Malle:maluisse,To haue oȝ had rather.

D   Conjugat Nolo.

M   Nolo,J will not,non-vis,non-vult: nolumus,non-vultis,nolunt.

Nolim,J might oȝ coulde nill, nolis, nolit: nolimus,nolitis, nolint.

Nolebam, J woulde not, nolebas, nolebat: nolebamus,nolebatis,nolebant.

Nollem,J might oȝ should nill, nolles,nollet:nollemus,nolletis,nollent.

Nolam, J shall be unwilling, noles, nolet: nolemus,noletis,nolent.

Noli oȝ nolito,nill thou:nolite oȝ nolito.

Nolui, J haue been unwilling, noluisti, noluit:

luit:noluimus,noluiſtis,noluerût oʒ noluere.

Noluerim, I might oʒ ſhould haue beene un-
willing,nolueris,noluerit:noluerimus,nolu-
eritis,noluerint.

Nolueram, I had beene un-willing,nolue-
ras,noluerat:nolueramus,nolueratis, noluerant.

Noluiſſem,I might oʒ ſhould haue had beene
un-willing, noluiſſes, noluiſſet:noluiſſemus,
noluiſſetis,noluiſſent.

Noluero,I ſhall oʒ will be un-willing,nolu-
eris,noluerit : noluerimus, nolueritis,nolue-
rint.

Nolle,to be un-willing, noluiſſe,to haue oʒ
had been un-willing.

D Conjugate Fero.

M Fero,I beare oʒ ſuffer,fers,fert : ſerimus,
fertis,ferunt.

Feram,I may oʒ can beare,feras,ferat:fera-
mus feratis,ſerant.

Ferebam,I did beare,ferebas,ferebat : ferebamus,ferebatis,ferebant.

Ferrem,I might oʒ ſhould beare, ferres,fer-
ret:ferremus,ferretis,ferrent.

Feram, I ſhall oʒ will beare, feres, feret: feremus,feretis,ferent.

Fer oʒ ferto,beare thou,ferto:ferte,ferunto.

Tuli,I haue boʒne,tuliſti,tulit: tulimus,tu-
liſtis,tulerunt oʒ tulere.

Tulerim,I might oʒ ſhould haue boʒne, tuleris

C

ris,tulerit:tulerimus,tuleritis,tulerint.

Tuleram,J had bo2ne, tuleras, tulerat: Tuleramus,tuleratis,tulerant.

Tulissem,J would o2 should have had bo2ne,
tulisses,tulisset: Tulissemus, tulissetis, tulissent.

Tulero,J shall o2 will beare, tuleris, tulerit:
Tulerimus,tuleritis,tulerint.

Ferre,to beare,tulisse,to have o2 had bo2ne.

Ferendi,ferendo,ferendum.

Latu,to be bo2ne,latum.

D Conjugat Feror.

Feror,J am bo2ne, ferris o2 ferre,fertur: ferimur,ferimini,feruntur.

Ferar,J may o2 can be bo2n,feraris o2 ferare,
feratur:feramur,feramini,ferantur.

Ferebar,J was bo2ne, ferebaris o2 ferebare,
ferebatur:ferebamur,ferebamini, ferebantur

Ferrer,J should o2 would be bo2ne, ferreris,
o2 ferrere,ferretur : ferremur, ferremini, ferrentur.

Ferar,J shall o2 will be bo2ne,fereris o2 ferere,feretur:feremur,feremini,ferentur.

Ferre o2 fertor,be thou bo2ne, fertor:ferimi-
ni,feruntor.

Ferri,to be bo2ne.

CAP. 6.

Of the second Conjugation in am.

D What

D *W*hat is the second Conjugation in *am*.

M   Whose second person singular of the first Present-tense finit, endeth in *is* or *iris*, with *i* long.

D Give an example of the first forme.

M Audio, I heare, audis, audit : audimus, auditis, audiunt.

Audiam, I may or can heare, audias, audiat: audiamus, audiatis audiant.

Audiebam, I did heare, audiebas, audiebat: audiebamus, audiebatis, audiebant.

Audirem, I should or would heare, audires, audiret: audiremus, audiretis, audirent.

Audiam, I shall or will heare, audies, audiet: audiemus, audietis audient.

Audi or audito , heare thou, audito: audite, or auditote, audiunto.

Audivi, I have heard, audivisti, audivit: audivimus, audivistis, audiverunt or audivere.

Audiverim, I should or would have heard, audiveris, audiverit: audiverimus, audiveritis, audiverint.

Audiveram, I had heard, audiveras, audiverat: audiveramus, audiveratis, audiverant.

Audivissem, I should or wold have had heard, audivisses, audivisset: audivissemus, audivissetis, audivissent.

Audivero, I shall or will heare, audiveris, audiverit : audiverimus, audiveritis, audiverint.

Audire, to heare, audiuisse, to haue oʒ has heard.

Audiendi, of hearing, audiendo, audiendum

Auditu, to be heard, auditum.

D Giue me an example of the second foʒme?

M Audior I am heard, audiris oʒ audire, auditur: audimur, audimini, audiuntur.

Audiar, I maye oʒ can bee heard, audiaris oʒ audiare, audiatur: audiamur, audiamini, audiantur.

Audiebar, I was heard, audiebaris oʒ audiebare, audiebatur: audiebamur, audiebamini audiebantur.

Audirer, I might oʒ should be heard, audireris oʒ audirere, audiretur: audiremur, audiremini, audirentur.

Audiar, I shall oʒ will be heard, audieris oʒ audiere, audietur: audiemur, audiemini, audientur.

Audire oʒ auditor, bee thou heard, auditor: audimini, audiuntor.

Audiri, to be heard.

Cap. 7.

Of an Adverbe.

D You haue shewed me woʒdes of number, now shewe me woʒdes without number?

M A woʒde without number, is that which signifignifieth no number.

D How many kindes are there of them?

M Two: an Aduerbe and a Conjunction.

D What is an Aduerbe?

M An Aduerbe is a worde without number, which is joyned to an other word, as valdè conſtans, diſſerit acutè, benè manè.

Therefore an Aduerbe is as it were an adjectiue, of Nounes, Uerbes, & Aduerbes them ſelues.

There are very fewe natiue Aduerbes. Vix, Cras, Heri, ita, non.

In like manner thoſe which are called Interjections, as Hei, heu, heus, ô, væ, pro, and eſpecially thoſe Prepoſitions, which are inſeperable from the word wherevnto they be joyned, as di, dis, re, ſe, am, Con, and theſe Prepoſitions which are ſeparable, as ad, apud, penes and the reſt.

Præ and Per, beeing compounded, increaſe the ſignification of the wordes vnto which they are joyned: as Perdoctus, prædiues.

Many Aduerbes come of Nounes not differing from the nounes, as are theſe nominatiues Vtrùm, multùm, minimùm, Potiſſimùm, as theſe Ablatiues, initio, veſpere, quo, qua, neceſſario, modo, and o being doubtful, ſero, ſedulo, mutuo, cito, crebro.

Secondly, Aduerbes are made of the Ablatiue caſe, which being diuers, they aduerbs are made diversely.

There bee manye ending in *im*, of the ablative of Substantives, as of Summa, summatim.

Some end in *itus*, as of fundo funditus. But there are very many, comming of the ablative of Adiectiues, ending in *o* or *i*, *o*, being changed into *é*, as of Docto, doctissime, docté doctissime.

But we say, bene, male, rite.

Sometimes *o* is chaunged into *itus* as divino, divinitus, or into *iter*, as firmo, firmiter, If the Ablatiue endeth in *i*, the adverb is made by putting to *ter*: as of acri acriter: forti, fortiter.

Adverbes comming of comparatiues, ende in *us*, as of doctiori, doctius, of fortiori, fortiùs.

Adiectiues ending in *ns* change *s* into *ter*, as of Amans, diligens, amanter, diligenter.

Also Adverbes of number, except semel, are made of nounes, as *bis*, for duis, ter, quater, quinquies, sexies, septies, octies, novies, decies, undecies, duodecies, tredecies, quaterdecies, quindecies, sexies-decies and sexdecies, deciessepties.

And furthermore Vicies, Tricies, quadragies, quinquagies, sexagies, septuagies, octogies, nonagies: so centies, ducenties, trecenties, quadringenties, quingenties, sexcenties, septingenties, octingenties, nongenties, millies

lies,ſo quoties,aliquoties,toties.

Also thoſe which end in *am*,as biſariam,triſa-
riam,quadriſariam,multifariam,omnifariam,
aliquotſariam, pridie,poſtridie,perendie,nu-
diuſtertius,nudiuſquartus: and ſuch like, and
are compounded of die tertio,quarto, that is
to ſay,it is the third daye,the fourth daye; and
they are alwayes ſayde of that which is paſt,as
Nudius-tertius dedi ad te epiſtolam.

CAP. 8.
Of a Conjunction.

D The laſt part of *Etymology* remaineth in x
   Conjuntion of the which laſtly, I aſk you
what you thinke?

M A Conjunction is a worde without number,
by the which the partes of a manifolde ſpeeche
are joyned togeather,it is eyther *Enuntiative* or
Ratiocinative.

D what is a conjunction *Enuntiative*?

M By the which the parts of a ſpeech are joi-
ned togeather.

They are partly congregatives, partly Se-
gregatives.

A Conjunction Congregative is that by the
which the partes are joyned together,as if they
were together true: And it is eyther a Copulative,or a Connexive.

A Copulative is by the which the partes are
4   abſolutely

abſolutely coupled together, as, ac, etiam, item, nec, quoque, que, and their Compoundes, atq; itemque, neque.

A connectiue, is that by which the partes following are knit by the condition of that going before, as ſi, ſin, ni niſi.

A Segregatiue is, by which the parts of ſpeech are diſſeuered, as if they were not togeather true.

And it is either a Diſcretiue or a diſiunctiue.

A Diſcretiue by which the partes by reaſon only are diſſeuered, as Autem, aſt, at, etſi, extraquam:interea, interim, vt, verò, verùm, nunc, tamen, etſi, tametſi, quanquam, quamvis, præterquam.

A Diſiunctiue by which the partes, are ſo ſeuered, as if one only could be true, as, aut, an, vel ve, ſiue, ſecus.

A ratiocinatiue, by which one part of the reaſon is as it were affirmed of the other part.

It is called a Cauſall, or a Rationall.

A Cauſall, by which, the cauſe of a thing going before is giuen, as enim, enimvero, etenim ſiquidem, quoniam, quia, quod, proptereaquod, nam, namque.

A Rationall, by which that following is concluded of that before, as Ergo, ita, itaque, igitur, ideo, quare, quamobrem, quapropter, quocirca.

The

The third Booke.

CAP. I.
Of the agreement of
Nounes.

D *Tymology* is declared with the partes thereof : nowe *Sintaxe* is to bee taught? What is *Syntaxe* ?

M *Sintaxe* is the seconde part of *Grammar*, which sheweth the construction of words, and it consisteth in Concorde of one worde with another, or in government of wordes.

D What is a Concorde?

M when the words do agree in common properties, which first of all is of wordes of number: as of a Noune with a Noune, and a Uerbe with a Noune: where note that many singular numbers are taken for a Plurall.

The Concord of a Noune with a Noune, is in number, Gender, and case : as Gravi teste privatus sum, amoris summi erga te mei, patre tuo clarissimo viro.

Here are three Substantives, Teste, Patre, viro, agreeing amongst themselues, in number, gender,

gender, and case: and likewise agreeing with their adjectives, Gravi, tuo, clarisimo in number, Gender, Case. Amoris, summi, mei, do also agree amongest themselues.

D What *Anomaly* is there of number?

M Either in Substantiues as Proclus & Eutisthenes reges: Celtebri, novus miles, or Adjectiues, as rex & regina beati.

D What *Anomaly* is there of Gender?

M It is eyther of one Gender vnlike to another, as Garumna flumine: animal quem vocamus hominem: Or of many Genders vnlike to one: where the masculine and the Feminine Gender of thinges that haue life, do agree vnto the masculine gender, as Pater & Mater mortui. But the diverse Genders of those thinges which haue no life, doe agree with the Neuter Gender, as Pulchritudo, constantia & ordo servanda sunt. The *anomaly* of Gender, and also of number is more seldome, as maxima pars vulnerati. The *anomaly* of case is most rare as Macte vir virtute esto: Macte for Mactus.

Cap. 2.

Of the Concord of a Verbe.

M HOwe is the Concorde of a Uerbe with a Noune.

M It is in number and person, ego, and nos are

are of the firſt perſon: tu and vos of the ſeconde perſon.

The Nominative Caſes of all other Nounes are counted of the third perſon.

Hereupon the Nominative of a Noune is called the ſuppoſit, and a Verb the Appoſit, as ego amo, nos amamus, tu amas, vos amatis, Tullius amat, tullij amant.

The *anomaly* of number is here leſſe uſual as: Cæpere quiſque.

The *anomaly* of perſons is moſſe continually in uſe. Nounes of the firſt, ſecond, and third perſon, joyned together, agree with a verbe of the firſt, as neque ego neque tu fecimus. Alſo Nounes of the ſeconde oꝛ thirde perſon joyned together, doe agree with a verbe of the ſeconde perſon, as tu & pater periclitamini.

CAP. 3.
Of the agreement of wordes without number.

DH Itherto we have heard the concoꝛde of woꝛdes of number.

The agreement of woꝛdes without number, how manifold is it?

M Two folde? of an Adverbe, and of a Conjunction.

An Adverbe is ſometime uſed foꝛ a Noune Relative,

Relative, as digna res eſt, vbi nervos intendas tuos, that it is to ſay, In qua. In like manner, Ille, ipſe, vnde, cauſa eſt cur: that is: quamobrem: multa ſigna dederat quamobrem reſponſurus non videretur.

Certain Adverbes of Comparison and number, have a peculiar agreement.

Quam, agreeth to every degree, as Quàm ſunt moroſi qui amant: perquam puerile.

And it either followeth one Comparative, or it is put betwixt two, as Tullius diſertior quàm Atticus: ſerius quam crudelius factum: with a ſuperlative, as habere quam laxisſimas habenas amicitiæ.

Vt is alſo joyned to the ſuperlative, as vt gravisſime diligentisſimeque potui.

Tam, ſometimes is of the ſame force, vituperanda eſt rei tam maximè neceſſariæ incuria.

Longè and multo agree to comparatives, and ſuperlatives, Longe melior, principi longe omnium gravisſimo. Multò commodiora: Conſpectus veſter multò jucundisſimus.

Adverbs ſignifying number agree to nounes Diſtributives, as bis, bina, ſeptenos octies ſolis anfractus.

CAP. 4.

Of the agreement of a Conjunction.

D The

D The agreeing of Conjunctions wherin is
it seene?

M In the order of going before, or of following, or of both.

Of Copulative conjunctions these go before,
Atq;, ac, et, sed, sedetiam, verum, verumetiam, nedum, nec, neq;, tum, quin, quinetiam.
Tali genere atq; animo. Parce ac duriter, Explosum & ejectum, and so in the rest.

This conjunction, &, from twenty to an hun-
dred, setteth in the former place the lesser number of nounes of number, as abhinc duos &
viginti annos est mortuus.

So doth it in Adverbes, as Proprium Catonis quater & quadragies causam dixisse.

Quoq; and que are onely set after, as Me scilicet maximè, proximè illum quoq;, fefellissent, Balbutire desinant, apertéq; audeant dicere.

These are common, etiam, item, itemq;, insuper, præterea, vel.

Of Connexives, si, ni, nisi, are common.

Sin, is onely set before, but all besides agree
with all Finitive-tenses or times. Si perfici-
unt optimè; Sin minus. Ni exeunt. Nisi ego in-
sanio.

Furthermore, there is agreement betwixte
this Conjunction and this Adverbe Fortè, as si
fortè. Nisi fortè.

Of Discretives these onely are set before, ast,
ar,

at,imo,sed,quòd,extraquã,præterquã,quam-
vis quanquam, Tu crebras à nobis literas expecta,aſt plures etiam mittito: nullum à vobis præmium poſtulo,præterquam hujus diei
memoriam ſempiternam &c.

Quanquam and quamvis agree to all Fini-
tive-tenſes,quanquam abeſt à culpa,ſuſpicio-
ne tamen non caret : quamvis ille fœlix ſit,
tamen,&c.

Theſe are ſet after:tantum,autem, interea,
interim,vero. Nil autem amabilius officijs.
Tum interea nullum veſtigium pecuniæ in-
uenietis,cum interim Scylla cum ijſdem ipſis
Ego vero Servi vellem.

Theſe are common, alioqui, alioquin, vt,li-
cet,tamen,porro.

Vt and licet agree onely to the ſecond ſinitive
tenſes.Vt illud non cogitares,tamen,&c.

All Diſjunctives are onely ſet before,as Aut
bibe aut abi, except ve, bis terve literas miſerat.

An is ſometimes a Diſjunctive, but an Interrogative. Erravit an potius inſanivit Apronius?

Of Cauſalls onely, Etenim,nam, namq; are
ſet before.Enim is onely ſet after.

Theſe are common, Enimvero,vt, vti,ſiqui-
dem,ne.

Of Rationalls theſe onely are ſet before, Sic,
quaſobres,quamobré,quapropter,quocirca.
　　　　　　　　　　　　　　　　Theſe

These are common, Ergo, ita, itaq;. Igitur is seldome set before: Igitur initio reges diversi pars ingenium, alij corpus exercebant.

The fourth Booke.

CAP. I.
Of the government of Nounes Substantives.

D Y Ou have shewed the concord of words: teach me now the government by the same way of teaching?

M Governement of words, is when one worde governeth an other with a certaine ende of varipng, which first of all shall be shewed in wordes of number, then after in Adverbes: and in words of number, the government of nounes both Substantives and Adjectives shall be first declared.

D How manyfolde is the government of a noune Substantive?

M Two folde. First: The substantive signifyng the thing adjoyned which is called an adjunct, governeth the Genitive case of the Substantive, signifyng the thing vnto which it is joyned called a subject, as Cato dicit

cit tanquam in PlatonisPolitia,non tanquam
in Romuli fæce sententia:here Plato is the subject to which Politia is joyned being an adjuct.
These Genitives,mei,tui,sui,nostrum,nostri,
vestrum,vestri,are used as subjectes : as Ratio
mei,nostri;defensor,tui.

A Gerund in *di*,is used as it were a Genitive
of the subject. Pueris non omnem licentiam
ludendi damus.

D Which is the seconde government of a
Substantive?

M A substantive of the subject or whole, serveth to the Genitive case,or Ablative of the adjunct,or part with an Adjective of praise or dispraise : Accipies hospitem non multi cibi,sed
multi ioci:virgo sparso ore,adunco naso.

Opus a substantive declined in one case, onely governeth an Ablative case,Authoritate tua
nobis opus est,consilio & gratia.

CAP. 2.

Of the government of Adjectives.

D The Governement of an Adjective
how manifold is it?

M Divers : but it is seene almost in quantitie or qualitie.In quantitie of degree,partition
and plentie.

The comparative degree governeth an Ablative case,Vilius argentum est auro,virtutibus
aurum.

aurum.

The Superlative degree governeth a Genitive case Plurall:Eloquentium iurisperitissi-
mus Crassus:iurisperitorum eloquentissimus
Scæuola.

A noune Adjective partative, governeth a genitive case,Quis est omnium his moribus.

An adjective of plenty or scarsenesse governeth a Genitive or Ablatiue,Plenus bonorum
& bonis.

D The governement of qualitie in which
doth it consist?

M In affinity,profit and desire.

An adjective of affinitie, or the contrary,go-
verneth a Genitive or Datiue case, as Affinis
suspitionis,& suspitioni.

An adjective of profite and the contrarye governeth a Datiue, as alicui cómodum,incom-
modum.

An adjective of desire governeth a genitive,
as amantissimus utriusq; nostrum: laudis cu-
pidus:studiosus doctrinarum.

Certaine adjectives governe the first Supine,
as Optimum factu.

Cap. 3.

Of the government of a Verbe
Active.

D   D Hitherto

D H Itherto the government of a noune is
declared: which is the government of a
Uerbe?

M It is first of a finit and personall verb, by
which sometime a noune, other somtime a verb
is governed.

D How manifold is it?

M Two folde : first or second : of the first government there is one only rule.

A Uerbe active governeth an accusative after him, as Fortem virum tibi commendo.

A verb Passive governeth an Ablative case: as
fortes creantur fortibus: but this government
is seldom without a Preposition. The Dative
is sometimes used for the Ablative : as senatui
non probatur.

Neuters and Deponents of them selues governe no case, as sedeo, loquor: notwithstanding they follow the government of the Active:
as Hæc cū loqueris nos Varrones stupemus:
currere cursum . Vtor, vescor, fungor, fruor,
gaverne an Ablative, as utor consilio tuo, fungor officio &c. Potior governeth an Ablative
or Genitive, as potior voto, potiri rerum.

Reminiscor, obliviscor, recordor, & memini, governe an Accusative or a genitive case, as
Oblivifcor lectionem or lectionis, reminiscor
historiam or historiæ &c.

CAP. 4.

CAP. 4.

Of the governement of a Verbe.

D **W**hat is the seconde government of a Uerbe?

M It is when an other case besides that first case is governed, and truely it is eyther simple or divers. Simple, as the Dative, the accusative, the Ablative.

A Uerbe by the force of acquisition governeth a Dative: as Suo sibi hunc jugulo gladio. But many Uerbes governe the same case, by a certaine germaine nature nor neare affinitie.

First Uerbes of comparison: as, se illis fere æquarunt.

Secondly, of giving or taking away: as Quæ victores civitatibus Siculis aut dederunt aut reddiderunt.

Thirdly, of commaunding, serving, declaring, promising, as cupiditatibus quibus cæteri serviunt imperare.

Fourthly, of resisting and the contrary, as Repugnare & resistere cupiditati. Cujus ego industriæ gloriæque faveo.

Fiftly, those verbes also have this governement of the Dative, which sometime are taken impersonally, as Nihil ei resistebat quod ipsis superat,

perat. Peccare licet nemini, Dolet mihi.

Cap. 5.

Of the government of Verbes of asking.

VErbes of asking, governe two Accusative Cases: as Illud te oro. &c.

In like manner, Moneo, consulo, cœlo, doceo. Qui nos nihil cælat, Quid te asine literas doceam?

Cap. 6.

Of the government of Verbes of plenty and price.

A Verbe of plenty and price, governeth an ablative case: of plenty, as saturire se sanguine: or the contrary, as spoliavit me bonis omnibus: Of price, as Mercari magno prætio.

Certaine Nounes are governed in the Genitive case, as Tanti, quanti, magni, pluris, maximi, plurimi, parvi, minoris, minimi, æqui, boni, flocci, Nihili, nauci, pili, assis, teruntij: depactus est tantidem, quanti fidem suam fecit; nihil tanti fuit.

Cap. 7.

Of the government of a Verbe Iudicial, and a Verbe Substantive.

A Uerbe judiciall governeth a Genitive or ablative case: as verbs of accusing and quitting: as Eam, tanquam capitis accusat, Absolvere improbitatis: crimine liberare: capitis arcessere.

A Uerbe substantive, or a verbe which obtayneth his force, governeth after him a Nominative taken for the same, as Tullius est Romanus: Beatisimi viuimus: but if the case following signifyeth possession, it shall bee put in the Genitive case. Erit igitur humanitatis vestræ.

But these possessives, Meum, tuum, suum, nostrum, vestrum are put for their Genitives, mei, tui, sui, Non enim est meum contra aliquem dicere.

If the same verbe be used for habeo, it governeth a Dative. Sunt mihi bis septem præstanti corpore nymphæ: but being used for afferre it doubleth the Dative, as Sempiternæ laudi tibi sit iste tribunatus, opto.

Cap. 8.

Of the government of a Verbe of deliberation and motion.

D I Understand how a Noune is governed of a
Uerb: How is a verb governed of a Uerbe?

M It is in Uerbes of deliberation and motion: a verb of deliberating governeth alwayes
an infinitive, as audeo, habeo, incipio, opto,
soleo, possum, propero, aggredior, molior, co-
nor, pigit, pænitet : as oblivifcor vigilare. Hoc
me memini dicere.

A Uerbe of mooving to a place governeth the
second supine. Admonitum venimus te, non
flagitatum.

A Uerbe of mooving from a place, doth som-
times governe the first supine : as obsonatu
redeo : cubitu resurgo.

Cap. 9

Of the government of a Verbe infini-
tive, and Impersonall.

D Now it is time to speak of the government
of a Uerbe Infinitive, and Impersonall.

M A verb Infinitive governeth an accusative
case before him: as men natu rumor est amare.

But after it, it governeth the case which the
finite Uerbe will governe, as Quapropter teipsum purgare ipsis coram placabilius est.

The last both Gerund and Supine being taken for the most part Impersonally, doe govern
also the case of their finit Uerbe, as aliqua consilia reperiendum est: but thou shalt speak that
ra-

rather by a gerund, except in Verbes Neuters
& Deponents, aliqua confilia reperienda funt.

The second Supine is very often used. Huic
quoque rei subventum eſt. But it obtayneth
only an active governmēt tō a verb of mooving
to a place. Cur te is perditum. Miſſa eſt ancilla
illico obſtetricem accerſitum, Neither is it
lawful at any time to ſay, Miſſum eſt ancillam.

The government of Imperſonals is proper
to ſome only: refert and intereſt, ſignifying profite oꝛ duty, govern a Genitiue caſe, as Illorum
retuliſſe videretur; reipub intereſſe putauit.

Except theſe ſeven Genitiues, Mei, tui. ſui,
noſtri, veſtri, noſtrum, veſtrum: foꝛ which theſe
poſſeſſives are vſed, as refert and intereſt mea,
tua, ſua, noſtra veſtra: Refert alſo and Intereſt
admit thoſe Genitiues of pꝛice and eſtimation,
tanti, quanti, magni, parvi.

In the reſt they have often, multum, plus,
plurimum, magis, minus, parvum, paululum,
pauxillum, aliquid, nihil.

Five Imperſonals miſerefcit oꝛ miſereſcit, oꝛ
miſeretur, tædet, piget, pænitet, pudet: govern
an accuſative of the thing, with a Genetive of
the ſufferer, as Me non ſolùm piget ſtultitiæ
meæ ſed etiam pudet: omnes noſtrimet nos
pœnitet.

CAP. 10

Of the government of Adverbes

D H Itherto was the government of wordes of
number declared: Shew hence forwarde
the government of adverbes?

M Derivatives govern such cases, as do their
Primatives·Nihilo minus. Omnium elegan-
tissimè, Naturæ convenienter & cōgruenter.

Adverbes of place governe a Genitive case,
Vbi terrarum esses: longe gentium.

These adverbes of time, as pridie, id est, pre-
cedente die:postridie, id est, postero die, haue
a threefoulde construction:pridie ejus diei:po-
stridie ejus diei: here is a Genetive:Pridie no-
nas:here is an accusative:Pridie quam excessit
è vita,is the third kinde of construction.

These adverbes of quantity,parum,satis,go-
verne a genitive : as Parum malæ rei:satis jam
verborum est.

Inlike maner do tantum, quantum, mul-
tum:en.ecce and o, govern a Nominative or an
accusative: as en hic ille est:en lectū: en tegu-
las:ecce autem Antonius : ecce miserum hominem: o consuetudo peccandi, o præclarum
custodem ovium.

Hei is either without case: or it governeth a
dative or a vocative : as hei vereor : hei mihi:
hei noster, laudo.

Heu governeth a Dative, an accusative, or a
Vocative:as Heu misero mihi: heu fuge nate,
dea: heu me infœlicem.

Heus governeth a Vocative,as heus Syre.

Væ

Væ governeth a Dative: as Væ capiti tuo .

Proh governeth an accusative oʒ Vocative: is proh deum atque hominum fidem: proh ancte Iupiter.

Thofe Adverbes which are called Prepofiti-ons, have a native fignification of place , but they ſerve often to times, perſons, and thinges.

Of thefe ſome governe one caſe onely, ſome two: they which govern one, govern an Accuſa-tive oʒ an Ablative.

Prepofitions governing an Accuſative caſe are thirty and one, Intra, extra, as Intra decem annos: extra oſtiū. Apud, penes, as apud me: Penes ſcenam exercitatus . Secus, ſecundū, as Naſcitur ſecus fluvios: Proximè & ſecundum Deos homines hominibus maximè vtiles. Iuxta prope, as Iuxta te ſū: propè montes, Ante, poſt, pone, as Ante oculos : poſt tergū : pone caſtra. Cis, citra, præter, vltra, trans, as Cis Eu-phratem: Citra Rhenum: Præter ripam: vltra modum: trans ripam. Inter, as Inter manus.

Erga, contra, as Erga te: contra veritatem.

Ad, vſq; , verſus, adverſus, as Ad focum : uſque Romam.

Verſus is alwayes ſet after: Adverſus there-of compounded is ſet befoʒe: as portum verſus: adverſus Deos.

Ob, per, propter. as Ob oculos : per totam caveam ire: propter tuum in me amorem.

Infra, ſupra, as Infra Saturnum : ſupra lunã.

Circa,

Circa,circum,circiter : as circa capuam : circum axem cæli:loca hæc circiter.

Prepositions which governe an Ablative case are fourteene. Præ,pro,coram, palam, tenus : as præ lachrymis : pro omnibus: coram genero meo:palam populo.

Tenus is alwayes set after:as tauro tenus.

De,ex,e,ab,ab,abs,absque and a. De,ex,ab, and absque are set before all letters : E and A, before Consonants onelye,as De maiestate : ex ære:e saxo:ab animo:abs quovis homine,absque te,a dicendo.

Abs is set before onely t and q : as abs quivis homine:abij abs te.

Cum,sine, as Cum exercitu:sine spe.

These Prepositions following governe an Accusative or an Ablative.An accusative with a Verb of moving:an ablative with a verb ofreff.

In with an accusative,as In vitam paulo serius,tanquam in viam ingressus.

But here the use is divers: as Ponere in oppido:ponere in possessionem.

In with an ablative , as In ære alieno multo esse.

Sub with an accusative,as Sub scalas se conjicere.

Sub with an Ablative , as homines sub terra habitantes.

Super & subter:as Super terræ tumulum:hac subter re:subter densa testitudine: subter præcordia.

cordia.

Procul: as procul muros: patria procul.

Clam: as clam patrem: clam js, whereupon commeth clanculum.

Uerbes beeing compounded with Prepositi-ons doe often keepe the case of the preposition, wherewith they be compounded, as te adeunt.

CAP. II.

Of the defecte of Præpositions.

D **D**Oth there remaine nothing of the go-verament of Prepositions?

M Truly oftentimes the preposition is wan-ting: whereupon also the government is called absolute: as in nounes of cause and of measure, and proper names of Townes.

A noune of cause is put in the ablatiue case: as Capitolium saxo quadrato substructum est: gloria clarus: authoritate gravis.

In like maner a noune of Instrument and of the maner of doing.

The speciall name of measure is oftentimes put in the accusatiue: sometimes also in the ab-latiue: as longū sesquipedem: latum pede: mu-ris ducentos pedes altis, quinquagenos latis.

The space of Time which is understood by quampridem, as a special name of measure, is put in the accusatiue: as ab hinc annos prope viginti.

In like manner that which is understoode by quamdiu : as, ubi per paucos dies commorabar.

Notwithstanding the terme of time which is understood by quando, is put onely in the ablative, as hora nona convenire cœpistis.

The proper name of a Toune is put in the accusative, if moving to a place be signified : or in the ablative, if the moving be by a place, or from a place, as cumas se contulisse dicitur. Iter Laodicia faciebam. Epistolas ad me Q. Servilius Tarso miserat.

If rest bee signified the proper name of a Toune beeing the singular number, and of equall sillables, is put in the genitive case : otherwise it is put in the Dative or ablative. Every one being of the plurall number, is put in the ablative: as Cum Laodiciæ, cvm synadis, cum Philomeli, cum Iconij: essem : fuisse Carthagini: Lacedemone esse presidium seneϴutis : audientem Cratippum idque Athenis.

A few not proper names of Tounes follow the same construction, as these accusatives, domum, rus : these ablatives, domo, rure: these genitives, domi, belli, militiæ, humi: and the Dative, ruri, as quorum virtus fuerat domi militiæque cognita: jacere humi: ruri habitare: rure jam redieram.

With these cases domi and domum, these
adjec

adjectives are joyned, mea, tua, sua, nostra, vestra, aliena: as me domo mea expulistis: nonne mavis sine periculo domi tuæ esse, quam cum periculo, alienæ?

D *What remayneth besides?*

M *The markes of points, put betwixt words, of which there are foure chiefe and principall, a *Subdistinction*, a *comma*, a *colon*, and a *period*.*

A *subdistinction* is by the which, that is distinguished which may serue by a little stape of breathing doubtfully to that going before, or following, and it is marked thus

A *Comma* is, by which with a little more staying, some sentence going before, is cut off from the perfection of that following, and it is noted thus ,

A *Colon* is, whereby a perfect sentence, but joyned with an other, is stayed with a lesse tyme of breath, and with the point put to the head of the letter, or els with two pointes it is thus noted

A *period* comprehendeth an absolute sentence, where the breath is altogeather stayed, the beginning whereof is noted with a great letter, and a point is set at the bottome of the letter thus . But there are peculier markes of marvailing thus ! Of asking a question thus ? A *parenthesis* is now distinguished with little strokes on both sides thus ( )

I have taught thee my Scholler the rudi-
ments

ments of Lattin Grammar, a moꝛe full and absolute knowledge whereof, is to be dꝛawne out
of these fountaines, from whence we have derived these little rivers. VVherefoꝛe when thou
shalt plainely perceive these, I wish thee learne
the others.

And I (best beloved Maister) will doe the
same with a chierefull desire.

In the meane time, foꝛ this I give you great
thankes, and will still gyve you as long as I
live.

FINIS.